The Last Laugh

March 2005

You crafty devil – you got the book.

You've just got one of the coveted copies of *The Last Laugh* competition book. Last year when we did a short story competition, called "End of Story", we only published 20,000 and they all went within about half an hour, so this time we've printed loads more.

The Last Laugh is just what we want BBC Three to be about: a smart idea, funnily done, which we hope people will love. It's part of our ethos at BBC Three to develop new talent. Not in a gym-subscribing-but-never-going, trackie bottoms kind of way. But by hiring ordinary people with extraordinary talent, from all walks of life and all ethnic backgrounds, with something to say which will entertain, inspire, move and tickle other members of the British public.

As a channel we've brought some great people on. In *Three Non Blondes* we hired three women, one of them straight from the check-out at Woolies and totally new to comedy, and commissioned them to do a very funny hidden camera series. We signed up Brian Dooley, an unknown writer with some experience of smoking in the smoking room of office blocks, to write something he knew lots about, and he came up with the hit BBC Three comedy *The Smoking Room*.

If you're famous and have just found this book whilst scrabbling through bins, then you may find more people than normal are staring at you in a funny way. That's because of the book love, not you. Even famous people get a chance on BBC Three. Julia Davies, a very funny actress and co-author of the brilliant *Human Remains*, wrote a very dark but extremely funny comedy called *Nighty Night*. And the boys who did BBC Three hit show *Little Britain* started somewhere and look where they are now. In big houses with no mortgage. And flowers. Flowers everywhere.

BBC Three also does award winning drama – hospital drama *Bodies* was ours, by new writer Jed Mercurio. Cop drama *Conviction* is also a BBC Three drama hit, as is the huge period drama *Casanova*, from the writer of *Queer As Folk*, Russell T Davies.

A big thing for us is parenting shows. On BBC Three we do toddler-training show *Little Angels*, the brilliant *Who Rules The Roost* and we've got a big series with world famous nanny Gina Ford coming up.

These are just some of the reasons why more people watch BBC Three than nearly any other digital channel. Tune in or, if you have any ideas, drop us a note. First though finish one of these sitcoms, and you too could have lots of flowers, and a downstairs toilet. Inside the house.

Stuart Murphy
Controller BBC Three
lastlaugh@bbc.co.uk

This book is published to accompany the BBC Three television series and sitcom writing competition "The Last Laugh".

Series Producer of "The Last Laugh" is Alison Black.

Published by:
The Last Laugh
BBC Scotland,
Queen Margaret Drive
Glasgow G12 8DG
First published 2005.

Paul Mayhew-Archer – Good Morning Miss Milton
Jesse Armstrong & Sam Bain – The Old Guys
Ian Brown & James Hendrie – Mike Davis, P.I.
Jonathan Harvey – Love For Sale
Carla Lane – Some Day I'll Find Me
Laurence Marks & Maurice Gran – Last Quango in Harris
Ian Pattison – Annie's People
Trix Worrell – Being Dad

The moral right of the authors have been asserted.

ISBN: 0 563 51943 6

Commissioning Editor: Stuart Murphy

Project Manger: Esther Coleman-Hawkins

Designer: ISO, Glasgow.

Text set in Century Schoolbook

Printed and bound in Great Britain by Martins of Berwick LTD

"The Last Laugh" Official Web Site www.bbc.co.uk/lastlaugh

The characters in the following sitcoms are fictitious. Any similarity to anyone living or dead is coincidental.

Contents

Good Morning Miss Milton

by Paul Mayhew-Archer

© Mike Prince

PAUL MAYHEW-ARCHER

Paul's first job was as a teacher but on the one school trip he organised he managed to get left behind. He then turned his hand to comedy where he became a producer of light entertainment at the BBC, producing award winning radio shows (Old Harry's Game and Delve Special) before settling as a script writer.

His most well known writing credits include The Vicar of Dibley and My Hero. He has also been a script editor on Spitting Image and was comedy script consultant for Channel 4. He is currently a consultant to the Head of Comedy at the BBC.

The title sequence shows children coming to school through the village – with their parents, on the school bus, in groups. The crucial thing – this village is beautiful, these children are happy. We would want to be at this school.

Each week the sequence ends with a different final image.

This week – we go past two children padlocking their bikes to see a girl tethering her pony.

SCENE 1

Int classroom. Day one. Morning. Location.

Miss Milton (Helen) is in her thirties and busying herself around her empty classroom – she is putting name cards on each table or desk to show where children should sit. she turns to camera as she does so.

HELEN   There are three ways to discipline a new class. You can spend the first half term slowly gaining their respect and establishing boundaries of acceptable behaviour. Boring or what? You can spend the first half term shouting and hitting them till you're suspended. Or you can try my method which takes ten minutes.

     (She looks over at the door) Ah here they come.

     Helen opens the door and starts to greet her class. They come in one at a time. She shakes their hand as they enter.

HELEN   Emma. Welcome to my class. I'm told you're really good at stories.

     Emma smiles at this compliment and passes

through.

HELEN   Simon isn't it? Welcome to my class. Mrs Lawrence says you're good at maths.

SIMON   I'm good at everything. Maths, English, sci –

HELEN   Super. What's 439 multiplied by 2,567?

(To cam as he goes off) That'll keep him quiet.

(Turns back to pupils) And you must be Madonna.

We see Madonna – she is wearing thick pebble spectacles and tries to shake hands with the wrong hand.

HELEN   Welcome to my class Madonna.

(Thinking on her feet) I'm told you're really excellent at smiling. Can you smile for me?

(Madonna beams) Perfect.

(As Madonna goes off Helen turns to cam) Spotted anyone who might get bullied in this class?

We see Madonna walking to her desk.

HELEN   *(To cam)* She might as well have a target pinned to her chest. She needs a safe haven.

A few moments later. the class are seated and Helen is at the front.

HELEN   Good morning 4M.

CLASS   Good morning Miss Milton.

HELEN   That's the ticket. First things first – I'm going to write my name down and I want you all to copy it onto your books.

A boy (Gary) flicks a pellet which hits Madonna in the back of the head. She yelps.

HELEN   Gary. I saw that. And if you do it again I shall call the Bogey man and have you taken away.

(There is some sniggering at this) I mean it. Right, so this is how my name is spelt. M. I.

Gary flicks at Madonna again.

HELEN   Excuse me one moment, class.

(She gets out a mobile phone and punches in a number) Hello, is that the Bogeyman? Yes I have a naughty boy in my class, Gary Marsh – I'd like you to come and remove him.

Thank you.

(Puts the phone away) Now as I was saying, it's M.I.L. You needn't bother with this, Gary, you won't be here long.

Gary looks worried. the others look puzzled.

HELEN   M.I.L.T.O.N.

The classroom door opens and a monstrous, deformed man-creature dressed in green enters – the Bogeyman.

BOGEYMAN *(His voice rasps)* Boy for the Bogeyman?

HELEN   *(Pointing)* That's right yes – that one there.

The Bogeyman goes to Gary and heaves him over his shoulder.

BOGEYMAN You're coming with me.

Gary shouts and struggles but the man takes him out. The rest of the class stare open-mouthed.

BOGEYMAN   Call me if you want any more taken.

HELEN   I will do, Mr Bogey. Thank you.

          (She turns to the class) Right class – if you'd like to sit up please.

          You've never seen a class sit up so well.

SCENE 2

Int. corridor. Day one. Morning. Location.

Helen walks along the school corridor, talking to us.

HELEN   See? Ten minutes and they're yours for life. A couple might be in therapy for life, but – well – you can't win 'em all.

          She passes the library door where we can see two excited children telling a third.

CHILD ONE   The bogey man just carried him off.

CHILD TWO   And he was huge, ten foot tall.

HELEN   *(To cam)* Ah. Sweet. Oh by the way, I should point out, he's not really the bogeyman. He's my cousin from Leicester. And the boy he carried off wasn't a real pupil. He's my nephew. I mention this because a teacher I know got hold of the wrong end of the stick and had one of her own pupils abducted. Very unfortunate. She's now working in Tescos, and her bogeyman's on the sex offenders register. Which I personally think is a bit harsh.

          Simon comes up.

SIMON   Miss Milton. One million, one hundred and twenty six thousand, nine hundred and thirteen.

HELEN   Excellent. And now divide that by the number
          of mats in the gym. See if you get the same
          answer as me..

          *He runs off. We're at the door marked
          "Staffroom".*

HELEN   This is the staffroom.

          (Suddenly leans into the camera) They're mad!

          She opens the door and:

SCENE 3

Int. staffroom. Day one. Morning. Studio.

*This is a bright cheery staffroom with comfy chairs, coffee
tables, notices on the wall and a sink in the corner with
coffee stuff (come into Dunmore juniors with me and I'll
show you). There are five women in the room, but we'll
only meet three. Linda Sweet (40 ish) is at her pigeon hole.
Wendy Youngblood (22) is sitting drinking coffee and
poring over a book, and Clare Tunney (late 20's) crosses
to Helen as she enters.*

CLARE   Helen. Saviour. I'm meant to be doing square
          roots with my class next and I was just
          wondering... what are they?

          Helen gives a look to cam.

CLARE   I've looked them up and I just do not get it.

HELEN   *(To cam)* This is the thing about teaching
          Juniors – you have to teach them everything,
          even though you only specialised in one
          subject. Clare specialised in PE. Everything
          else –

(She does that "way over the head" gesture. then turns to Clare) – Each number is the square of another number multiplied by itself.

(Clare looks blank) So for instance four is two multiplied by two. So Four is the square of two. And so two is the square root of four.

(To cam as Clare stares) If she was in hospital they'd be switching the life support off around now.

CLARE   So what's the square root of two?

HELEN   Ah well then you're into decimals.

CLARE   Oh no. Not decimals please. Please not d...

HELEN   Clare, you've got to do decimals sometime.

CLARE   I can't.

HELEN   You've got to.

CLARE   Oh God. I'm getting all sweaty just thinking about it.

HELEN   *(Opening her case)* Look here's a worksheet. Just give them that.

CLARE   Thanks, Helen.

HELEN   Courage mon brave...

        (Clare looks blank) It's French.

        They are distracted by the off-screen sound of Linda clapping her hands and calling.

LINDA   *(Barely suppressed rage)* Excuse me everyone.

(We see Linda by the sink) Everyone, if I could have your attention for one moment please. I have an important announcement. My mug is missing. My blue mug. That is my mug and someone has removed it.

HELEN *(To cam)* The two most serious crimes a teacher can commit are a) Killing a pupil and b) Using another teacher's mug. And b is the biggie.

LINDA *(Shaking)* I don't know who and I don't know why but I cannot take much more of this.

HELEN *(Crossing to her)* It's all right Linda.

LINDA Life's hard enough as it is, Helen, without this.

HELEN I know, I know.

LINDA I've got an impossible job, the most difficult class in the school.

HELEN You've got the infants Linda. They're five.

LINDA Exactly. Five year old animals. They run around, they won't sit still. Two of them are in nappies. They're five for God's sake.

HELEN I know.

LINDA I'm a teacher, I'm not meant to do nappies.

HELEN There, there, it's all right.

Wendy comes up with a blue mug.

WENDY Sorry. Is this your mug?

HELEN *(To Linda as to a child)* There you are, Linda. There's your mug.

Linda takes it like a comfort blanket.

WENDY Sorry. I didn't realise.

LINDA One more thing like that and, believe me, I'll tip right over.

 (Turns to Wendy) I've left my prozac at home, can I have one of yours?

WENDY I'm not on Prozac.

LINDA But you're a teacher.

WENDY Well yes, but... I'm not on Prozac.

LINDA You soon will be.

 Linda goes off to get her coffee. Helen turns to Wendy.

HELEN Thanks. You must be Wendy. Cherry's replacement.

WENDY *(Nods indicating Linda)* Is she ok? She doesn't seem to like children. Sorry, I just cannot understand that.

HELEN *(Turns to cam)* At last – a sane teacher.

WENDY Children are angels in human form, sent from our good Lord above.

HELEN *(To cam)* Spoke too soon.

 The staffroom opens and Colin Sawyer, the headteacher (mid 40's, fancies himself) enters.

COLIN Right. Ladies. I just have a couple of notices.

 (Linda is busy with her coffee. He leans across.) If I could just have your attention for a –

LINDA I'm getting a coffee!

COLIN Right. Right. First I'd like to welcome our new member of staff – Miss Youngblood.

Wendy smiles.

This is Miss Youngblood's first job and as we all know the first three years of teaching are the worst – a complete and total nightmare – so best of luck. You'll need it.

He smiles at her. She's now not smiling.

COLIN And second – in accordance with LEA guidelines, please remember this is an open school. Parents and prospective parents can come in at any time. I try to stop them, but the bastards sneak in anyway. So please look as if you know what you're doing. Also, one of the things prospective parents like to see is pupils' work up on the walls. So let's impress them eh? From now on I only want the work of bright pupils up there.

(Helen stares) Low achievers – say well done and lock it in a drawer. And if you don't have enough bright pupils I have some excellent work from other schools which you can stick up instead.

(He holds up a sheaf of children's work.) Right. That's all.

He goes. Helen turns to the others.

HELEN Work from other schools????

CLARE Brilliant.

(Going) I'll see what he's got.

LINDA — Well I'm sorry, I think it's a bloody cheek

(Helen looks relieved) Expecting us to stick up children's work. I'm a teacher not a decorator.

(Going off) I've never stuck up work and I am not starting now.

HELEN — Wendy, what do you think?

WENDY — He is so wrong. All pupils' work should be celebrated whatever their ability.

HELEN — Exactly.

WENDY — Even if it's a scrawl or a squiggle – or even just a blob on the paper – it's the work of a child, one of God's little miracles.

HELEN — No – losing it now.

WENDY — And we should stick it up. Who are we to sit in judgement on children?

HELEN — We're teachers. It's our job.

(To cam) I know what you're thinking. Why don't I work in a normal school? Believe me, this is a normal school. Mind you, I sometimes wonder why I stay.

The staffroom door opens and Ben Lovett, the caretaker, enters. He is mid twenties and deeply, ruggedly handsome. We see him as Helen sees him – in a shimmery golden haze, moving in slow motion and accompanied by that Diet Coke music. Helen's eyes follow him as he comes up.

HELEN — *(To cam)* And then I realise – I stay for the kids. Obviously.

BEN *(He has a lovely attractive burr)* Morning Helen.

(Helen gulps) Would you be Miss Youngblood?

WENDY I would, yes.

BEN Ben Lovett, caretaker. I understand how as you was telling your class how God calls people to do things.

WENDY *(Pleased)* That's right, God called me to be a teacher, you see.

BEN I got a lad outside says God's calling him to go home. I caught him getting on the bus.

WENDY Ah, the poor child's misunderstood the –

BEN And when I stopped him he told me to eff off and said God called him to say it.

WENDY I'll speak to him right away.

BEN So I clipped him round the ear and brought him back.

WENDY You struck a child?

BEN God called me to do it.

Wendy looks at Ben uncertainly.

WENDY Right. Right.

She goes.

HELEN *(A reproving look)* Ben.

BEN It was only a tap. Anyway Jesus said it's ok to hit children.

HELEN Did he???

BEN	Yeah, he talked about making children suffer.
HELEN	No. No, that's 'suffer little children'. It doesn't mean that at all.
BEN	Oh. I thought it did. Well he caught me at a bad moment.
	I'm a bit wound up.
HELEN	Oh. I'm sorry.
BEN	You know my girlfriend, Lucy. How devoted I've been. I mean I haven't so much as looked at another woman in the last two years.
HELEN	*(With feeling)* No, I know.
BEN	Well – she's walked out on me.
HELEN	*(Trying to sound convincing)* No! Oh God. Ben. That's awful. You poor thing.
BEN	I did everything for her. She wanted me to be super fit so I got super fit. I mean you have to work to get pecs like these.
	He flexes his muscles.
HELEN	*(Staring at them)* I'm sure you do.
BEN	They don't come easy. Have a feel, go on..
	(She is reluctant) Go on, have a feel.
HELEN	*(Tentatively feeling them)* Mm. Yes. I see what you mean.
BEN	That is solid muscle, that is. That is hours of training. That is me in the bedroom in nothing but a pair of Y fronts doing pressups till my entire body's aching and glowing like it's on fire.

HELEN   *(Almost breathless)* I can imagine.

BEN   And it's not just pecs either. There's this as well.

(He taps his abdomen) And this. *(He turns so she can admire his bum)*

She wanted a bloke with a great bum so I got a great bum. I mean, tell me this isn't a great bum.

HELEN   Well... er...

BEN   Go on, have a feel, then tell me it isn't.

Helen looks around to see anyone is looking but they've all gone.

BEN   Go on. Please. I need to know.

Helen places her hand tentatively on his bum and moves it up and down.

HELEN   ... Yep...seems pretty great to me.

BEN   Yeah but not to my Lucy.

(We cut to his face as he remembers) No, she'd rather run off with some sodding farm hand when it comes down to it, leaving me high and dry. I don't know what to do, Helen. I mean, what do you think I should do?... Helen?

Another angle shows that Helen is lost in a reverie with her hand on his bum.

HELEN   *(Removing her hand)* Sorry, I was miles away. What did you say?

BEN   What should I do?

HELEN   Well – you've been hurt, you've been
               wounded... you should hurl yourself into
               another relationship at the earliest
               opportunity.

BEN   Should I?

HELEN   Today if possible.

BEN   Today??

HELEN   Yes. With an older woman. Preferably
               someone you know and like.

BEN   Blimey. Who?

HELEN   *(Tossing her hair)* Ooh I don't know. Let's
               think.

               (She licks her lips seductively)... Erm...

BEN   There's Clare I suppose.

               *We see Clare enter and get her bag from her
               chair.*

BEN   She's pretty.

HELEN   Yes. If you like that sort of vacant air-heady
               prettiness.

BEN   Yeah I love it.

HELEN   Right. Right.

BEN   But the thing is I don't really know her.

               (Thinking) Come to think of it, the only person
               I really know – and like – is you. I don't
               suppose you'd consider... erm...

HELEN   Me? Good Lord. Ben. I wasn't expecting this.

BEN	Sorry, I shouldn't have suggested it. It's only because I'm desperate.
	(Helen gives him a look)
	No. Not desperate. Obviously. I mean confused. Lost. Insane.
HELEN	Shut up.
BEN	What I mean is I like you, but I would never normally have –
HELEN	I know what you mean. And – well – as it happens I'm not seeing anyone at this moment in time... so...
BEN	You're desperate as well.
HELEN	No. Of course I'm not desperate, don't be ridiculous, I'm just happy to be a comfort in times of need.
BEN	*(Nods)* You are desperate aren't you.
HELEN	More desperate than you can imagine.
	She kisses him. They clutch at each other furiously as they disappear into a corner of the room behind some shelves.
HELEN	*(Between kisses)* Not now. I'm teaching in three minutes.
BEN	Where?
	(Kiss) When?
HELEN	Year Four. In three minutes. I just –
BEN	No, I mean...
HELEN	*(Realising)* Oh. After school. Anywhere but my place.

BEN   Why? What's wrong with your place?

HELEN   *(Looks to cam)* It's also my mother's place. She's an invalid and I just don't think she wants me to meet anyone and leave her. Last time I took someone home – two years ago – she kept banging her stick on the wall shouting "stop it, stop it now, you dirty girl".

          (To Ben) I live with my mum. She'd get in the way.

BEN   *(Alarmed)* She'd want to join in?

HELEN   No. No. She'd just get in the way.

BEN   How about my cupboard, four pm?

HELEN   Perfect.

BEN   I'll get a mat, and shift the mop and bucket I use to...

HELEN   Too much detail.

          The bell goes.

          Four it is.

SCENE 4

Int. classroom. Day one. Afternoon.

Helen is with her class. She looks at the clock – it's 3 pm.

HELEN   Right. I like to end each day by reading a book.

          (They look excited) Before I start, can anyone tell me the name of a good story writer?

          All hands shoot up.

HELEN   Emma.

EMMA   Joanne Rowling.

HELEN   Good. Anyone else? Tom?

TOM   J.K. Rowling.

HELEN   Ye-es That's the same person isn't it. Any other good story writers?

They all look puzzled except Madonna. She puts her arm up.

HELEN   Madonna.

MADONNA   The lady who writes Harry Potter.

HELEN   Right. Yes. Pattern emerging now. OK, let's try something else. Can anyone tell me the name of a good book...

All hands go up.

Without the name Harry Potter in the title?

All hands go down except for Simon's.

Simon.

SIMON   "Quidditch Through the Ages".

HELEN   Excellent. That's perfect. Well you'll be pleased to know that the book I'm going to read is all about a young wizard.

They excitedly whisper "it's Harry Potter".

Called "The Wizard of Earthsea"

She holds the book up. The children groan. We hear a "not Harry Potter?"

HELEN   No, not Harry Potter.

The class groan.

But another boy wizard who goes to wizard school, has all sorts of exciting adventures and learns spells

They're not interested.

And finally meets Harry Potter.

They all sit up excitedly.

HELEN *(To cam)* OK. He doesn't. But he will in my version.

(Starts reading) "It was on the Island Of Roke in the middle of Earthsea that a boy named Ged was born".

EMMA When does he meet Harry?

HELEN Later!

SCENE 5

Int. the classroom. Day one. A bit later.

Helen is putting up work on the classroom wall – maps of the world which they have coloured in and labelled. She looks at the clock – it's 3.30. Madonna has stayed behind and comes up.

MADONNA Miss Milton.

HELEN Yes Madonna

MADONNA Emma says you're going to send me to the bogeyman because I'm thick.

HELEN *(Sympathetic)* Oh Madonna, that's rubbish with a capital rur. I only send naughty children to the bogeyman, not thick ones, so you've nothing to worry about.

	(Realises)... not that you're thick anyway. You have a lot to offer and anyone who says you're thick is triple thick with added thickness.
MADONNA	My mum says I'm thick. Is she triple th–
HELEN	Except your mum, obviously. You are not thick – as this super map of the world you've done clearly shows... why have you made the sea all red?

She shows Madonna (and us) the map with the seas all coloured red, and all the land coloured green.

MADONNA	You told us to. You said put in the red sea.
HELEN	Right. Right. Yes. Hence all the green land as well. Actually the Red sea's not a colour, it's a name –

(Pointing to map) It's the name of this little sea here.

MADONNA	Next to France.
HELEN	No. Next to – well yes, next to France on your map, but that should be Egypt. France should be over here, where you've got China.
MADONNA	Sorry Miss Milton.
HELEN	No, no. Don't be sorry. I should have explained it better. Tell you what.

(Rubbing out and writing in) If we just change these few names around. Like so. Very clever of you to write the names in pencil so I can rub them out.

MADONNA	I had to – I was chewing my pen and I swallowed the nib.

HELEN   Right. So, like I say, if we just change these
             round – then voila! It's good enough to go up
             on the wall.

             (Pinning it up) Have you had work up on the
             wall before?

MADONNA   *(Shakes her head)* I've not been in this room
             before.

HELEN   No, no, I mean up on any wall.

             (Madonna shakes her head again) Well you
             have now. And if anyone asks you why the
             sea's all red just say shark attacks.

SCENE 6

Int. store cupboard. Day one. Four pm.

*Ben is in the store cupboard. It's a large windowless
walk-in cupboard the size of a small study. It's cluttered
with caretaking stuff. There is a gentle tap on the door
from outside and he lets Helen in.*

HELEN   Ben. About this morning. It was great – really
             – but this little voice in my head keeps telling
             me I –

             He kisses her. She kisses him back. Then.

BEN   Sorry, what does the little voice keep telling
             you?

HELEN   I've no idea, It's too little. I thought you might
             have gone off the idea.

BEN   *(Shakes his head)* I picked you some flowers.

             *He indicates some flowers in the mop bucket –
             he's placed the stems in the holes where you
             squeeze the mop.*

HELEN *(Touched by his efforts)* Aah. Thank you. Nice idea. They should do that on Changing Rooms.

BEN And I put a J cloth over the light to make it more romantic.

There is indeed an orange J cloth over the light bulb.

Bit basic I know, but –

HELEN It's perfect. I feel like Mimi in La Boheme. Not when she's dying, obviously. But earlier.

BEN And I got this barrel of creosote out of the shed.

HELEN Bloody hell, what are you planning?

BEN For you to sit on.

HELEN Oh right. Right. Sit on.

BEN I'll get a mat. I would have got one earlier but there was some boy in the gym, counting them.

HELEN Some very weird children in this school.

Ben turns to go then turns back and kisses her.

BEN Has anyone ever told you you're lovely?

HELEN No-one over seven years old.

He goes. She goes all gooey and looks at the camera.

HELEN God, I think I'm in love. My tummy's all churned up and I can't stop shivering – so either I'm in love or I've got flu and wind at the same time.

(She burps) Oh no. Please don't let me burp in his face. That would not be attractive

She looks at herself in the cracked mirror on the wall.

HELEN I look terrible.

She tries to rub some colour into her lips, then gets a red marker biro out of her bag and applies that and rubs her lips together to spread the ink.

HELEN That's better.

There is a tap on the door. Helen opens it.

HELEN *(Sexily)* That was quick. Do you do anything slowly?

It's Simon.

SIMON Try not to, Miss. Mum says I'm quick at everything.

Helen stares

I've got the answer to that question.

HELEN Good.

(Closing the door) Bye.

SIMON *(Opening it)* It's twenty five thousand and forty two point five.

HELEN Yes, that's what I made it. Bye.

(She closes then opens the door) How did you know where to find me?

SIMON I saw you go in. That's another of my skills – noticing things. I'm going to be a policeman when I grow up.

HELEN   That's something we can look forward to.

SIMON   What shall I do now?

HELEN   Go away.

SIMON   No, I mean what shall I work out?

HELEN   How many feet it is from here to your home. Starting now.

SIMON   OK. Bye.

He starts to go, counting the feet as he walks off.

SIMON   Shall I come back and tell you when I've done it?

HELEN   No.

He goes. Colin, the headteacher, appears in the doorway.

COLIN   Ah Helen.

HELEN   Oh God.

COLIN   Glad I've caught you.

(Lowers his voice) Is Mr Lovett there?

HELEN   *(Wary)* No. Why?

COLIN   Good.

(He joins her in the cupboard) A discreet word. Apparently his girlfriend has just dumped him.

HELEN   Oh dear.

COLIN   Yes. Crying shame. If she'd dumped him a month ago, he'd have had the holidays to get over it. Anyway, the thing is –

	(He notices something) Is that a J cloth?
HELEN	Oh yes. How peculiar.
COLIN	Hmm. And he's got a bouquet in his bucket.
HELEN	Maybe it's the break up. It's sent him a bit odd.
COLIN	Yes, well – that's what I wanted to talk about. I think this break up could cause problems.
HELEN	*(Wary)* Really?
COLIN	I've been thinking – handsome young caretaker on the loose, before long he'll be after one of my attractive young teachers... So I want you to keep an eye on Clare and Wendy.
HELEN	... Clare and Wendy, right.
COLIN	You and Linda needn't worry, you'll have no trouble with him at all – but Clare and Wendy... well they are pretty aren't they.
HELEN	Yes. They are pretty.
COLIN	And they need protecting. This is a school not Carry on Caretaker. So if he makes a move you get in his way.
HELEN	*(Very definite)* Don't you worry, I'll be all over him
COLIN	Good. Because I do not want any hanky panky going on. That's why I've always resisted the temptation myself.
HELEN	With the caretaker?

COLIN   No – obviously not with the caretaker! With
             members of staff. Believe me, that's been quite
             a struggle, the amount of temptation I get.

HELEN   *(Finds this hard to believe)* Really?

COLIN   Oh don't play the innocent Helen. I've seen
             the looks you and Linda give me. I know you
             both find me attractive.

             (Helen looks amazed) But I've never responded
             because I knew it would lead to trouble.

HELEN   You're right there. What sort of looks?

COLIN   Oh little smiles – little come hither glances.
             You're probably not even aware you're doing
             it.

HELEN   No. I'm not.

COLIN   But you do it subconsciously. I've obviously
             got some sort of magnetic appeal or
             something. I get the same looks from most of
             the mothers. In fact from most women I meet.

HELEN   Rrright. And you're quite sure these looks
             mean they find you attractive.

COLIN   Oh yes. Yes, definitely.

             (Looks at her) You're doing it now. That little
             frown. Very come hither.

HELEN   Rrright.

COLIN   But don't worry. I shall resist.

HELEN   Good.

COLIN   Because – as we both know – you cannot
          conduct a relationship in front of three
          hundred nosy children. It undermines your
          authority as a teacher.

HELEN   *(The truth of this hits home)* Yes. Yes, I
          suppose it would.

COLIN   So – see you tomorrow. And regards to your
          mother.

HELEN   Thank you.

          *He goes. Helen sighs. Then the door opens
          again and Ben is there with a mat.*

WHAT HAPPENS NEXT?
CAN YOU HAVE THE LAST LAUGH?

GOOD MORNING MISS MILTON BY PAUL MAYHEW ARCHER

The Old Guys

by Jesse Armstrong & Sam Bain

© Mike Prince

JESSE ARMSTRONG & SAM BAIN

Jesse and Sam met at Manchester University on a creative writing course. Since then they have written for a number of sketch shows including Smack the Pony and 2DTV and children's sitcoms such as My Parents Are Aliens.

Peep Show, of which they are co-creators and associate producers, is their first original sitcom to make it to TV. Two series have been produced so far for Channel 4. The first series won the Rose D'or for Best Comedy Show 2003 and was nominated for Best Comedy by BAFTA and the Royal Television Society. A pilot for a US version of the show is currently being made by Carsey Werner for Fox TV.

SCENE 1

Int. Café. Day. (Day 1).

Tom and Roy are sitting at a window table in a greasy spoon watching the world go by.

TOM   Look at it Roy. Look at it all. The whole, filthy, fantastic mess we've made of it all.

ROY   Heh, quite the sight isn't it Tom? 'The modern world.'

TOM   *(Re: passers-by)* Great hairy gorillas with Burberry baseball caps. Dribbling loonies walking the streets free as birds... lovely young ladies showing off their wares like the world's one enormous bordello.

ROY   'Caught in that sensual music all neglect/ Monuments of unageing intellect.'

         (Beat) W.B. Yeats.

         Roy looks pleased with himself.

TOM   There's no need to bring poetry into it Roy, I'm just saying. *(Beat)* Jesus. Just because it was written by 'W.B. Yeats' you want me to sit up and bark like a dog?

ROY   I just thought...

TOM   *(Cutting him off)* Yes well.

         They sit in silence for a beat.

TOM   *(Cont.)* So what shall we do later? Catch a matinee? Road Trip 2's probably still playing somewhere – worth another spin don't you think?

ROY   (*Checks watch*) Actually, I'm afraid I've got to
         be going soon, I'm off to have lunch with Pen.

TOM   (*Disappointed*) Penny? Your ex? Why are you
         going to see that drug addled bag of...

ROY   I don't know why you're always suggesting...
         she was never taking 'ludes', it was HRT.

TOM   Hey, don't blame me, I'm not the crazy who
         sewed all your ties to your shirt collars.

ROY   In many ways that was a brilliant time-saving
         idea.

         (*Beat*) Anyway, she's been sending me quite a
         few positive signals. A birthday card, for
         example. Signed just by herself – no Des, see?
         Encouraging eh?

TOM   (*Shaking head*) Tsch. Oh Roy.

ROY   (*Getting up*) You can 'tsch' all you like but I
         think it's going to be fun. We're going to a
         restaurant on a barge. All going well, I
         thought I might read her some Kipling.

TOM   Restaurant on a barge – Kipling? I'm sorry
         Roy but you've just hit a new low.

ROY   Tom, don't go like that. I know you don't like
         being left on your own, but you'll be alright
         old pal. I'll be back by five.

TOM   (*Bristling*) No need to 'old pal' me, friend. I'll
         be fine. Oh yes, no need to worry about me.
         I'm going to be more than fine.

ROY   Yes. Well. Just don't go down to Caesar's
         World okay? You know how you get once you
         start working your 'system' on the fruitie.

TOM No danger, no danger Roy. While you're chomping away on a drumstick quoting Mr Kipling I'm going to be living it up. To the max.

ROY Well it would be ideal if you're out, because I was thinking if things get... *(Looking around, self-conscious)* saucy, Penny and I might head back to the house.

TOM Oh please!

ROY Could happen. Could very easily happen.

TOM Oh sure! Sure it could.

  (Explaining to an idiot) Nothing's going to happen Roy.

ROY Listen Tom I know how you feel about the possibility of me living a, ahem, 'full' life when yours is a bit 'empty' in that department but...

TOM Roy, you can stop right there. Alright? Because you know what I'll be doing this afternoon? Do you? Do you actually know? Can you even imagine?

ROY No.

TOM *(Busking it)* Exactly. Cos I'll be – doing it. The actual it. Getting it. While you're quoting on about fondant fancies on your barge I'll be having an actual piece of pie.

  (Beat) Sex – pie.

ROY *(Wry)* Right, and with whom are you going to be eating sex pie exactly? One of the women from the mobile library? Wendy Martin perhaps?

TOM   *(Disgusted)* No not bloody Wendy from the
       mobile library. Roy I'm a bohemian – there are
       more things in my... universe than you can
       conceive of ...

       (Beat) Look - I'm going to be eating sex pie
       with a, a

       (Under his breath)... gorgeous young
       prostitute.

ROY   *(Under his breath, embarrassed)* A prostitute?
       You're going to see a prostitute?

TOM   It's perfectly natural Roy, it's what everyone
       does these days. It's filthy, it's fun, it's
       everything you want and everything you hate
       all wrapped up together in one lovely dirty
       package.

ROY   Blimey. Okay.

TOM   *(Pleased with what he's come up with)* Yes
       'Blimey'. Yes 'Okay'. Exactly. Puts everything
       into perspective doesn't it? That's the kind of
       roister doister you're dealing with here Roy.

SCENE 2

Int. Roy and Tom's flat. Day. (Day 1).

*Tom sitting on his own looking bored, playing a game by
himself – 'Ker-plunk.' He 'wins'.*

TOM   *(Triumphant)* Ha ha!

       *Then he settles back in his seat looks bored.
       fidgets for a beat, tries to get comfortable. looks
       over at the phone. Idly picks it up. Dials.*

TOM   *(Cont.) (After a beat, into phone)* Hello, yes,
           I was wondering if you could tell me what's
           new out this week.

           (Beat) No, nothing in particular, I have
           extremely broad taste.

           (Beat) All right, what about... fresh produce.
           Or ready meals. What's new in ready meals?

           *A key can be heard in the door, Tom hangs
           up abruptly. Tom's daughter Amber
           (30's, unsettled, chirpy) enters.*

AMBER   Hi Dad. I was hoping you'd be in. I want to
           have a long chat with you.

TOM   *(Depressed)* Ohhhh. Have you been 'thinking
           about things' again?

AMBER   Yes. And guess what? I've started going to
           church! I really feel that things are looking up
           for me.

TOM   *(Looking at paper, distracted)* I thought things
           were already looking up for you, with the
           pottery class. I thought pottery was going
           to make everything all right?

AMBER   Oh great. Thanks Dad.

TOM   What?

AMBER   Chip chip chip, always chipping away with
           your little chisel aren't you?

TOM   No. What? What are you talking about?

AMBER   You and your chisel, undermining me.

TOM   I have no chisel, there is no chisel.

AMBER   Look, never mind, forget it. That's the family speciality isn't it? Anyway, I think you should come along.

TOM   Church? I'm not coming to church. That is just not going to happen Amber.

AMBER   It's not church, it's The Pathway Course.

TOM   Yeah, but it's in church, isn't it? It's not being held down the multiplex.

AMBER   I just think it would be a very good for you and me to do something together.

TOM   Well, of course, let's go for a snifter.

AMBER   Not alcohol Dad, the answer to everything isn't at the bottom of a pint pot.

TOM   Well it ain't in the Bible either, and I know where it's more fun looking.

AMBER   It might help heal some of the wounds that happened during my childhood.

TOM   Oh sure, I get it, just because your mother's in the ground suddenly she's Little Miss Perfect.

AMBER   Look, Dad, all I'm saying is that it would be great, for me personally, to use this as an opportunity to forgive you.

TOM   You can't forgive me because I don't want to be forgiven. Anyway I didn't do anything wrong.

AMBER   I can forgive you. I'm going to learn to forgive you.

TOM   No you can't. I won't let you.

AMBER   I might start now in fact. I'm going to forgive you.

TOM   Bollocks.

Tom folds his arms, looks at Amber triumphantly.

TOM   *(Cont.)* Go on, try it again. Try to forgive me. Just try it. Go on.

SCENE 3

Ext/int. Church hall. Day. (Day 1).

Amber and an uncomfortable-looking Tom are approaching the side door of a church.

AMBER   Thanks a lot for coming Dad. It means a lot to me.

TOM   *(Covering any emotion)* Yes, well, there's no need to go on about it, it doesn't mean that much. If they'd stop buggering about with the Bergerac times, I'd still be at home.

AMBER   You know it's all right to admit you might actually have some love for your own daughter. There's nothing 'soppy' about that.

TOM   *(Surly, childish)* So you claim.

Tom follows amber into a church hall. There is a circle of eight or so people, including Phil the Reverend, sitting on plastic chairs.

REV PHIL   Hi there. I'm Reverend Philip Jenner. And thank you all for coming up the 'pathway' to this first session of the Pathway Course.

Tom and Amber take their seats.

REV PHIL   *(Cont.)* We usually kick off by encouraging everyone to introduce themselves and say a few words about what brought them here.

Phil looks at Amber.

AMBER   Er – I'm Amber – and I, well I feel like I've been on a long journey, but the Church, feels, I suppose, like coming home.

REV PHIL   *(Looking into her eyes)* I know exactly what you mean and I think it's very beautifully put.

Phil looks at Tom sitting to his left, smiles encouragingly.

REV PHIL   How about you?

TOM   *(Squirming)* Me? I'm here for the hamper.

Reverend Phil smiles indulgently and looks at Tom, expecting him to continue.

TOM   *(Cont.)* There is a hamper isn't there?

(To Amber) You weren't shitting me about the hamper?

REV PHIL   No, no, that's right, there's a free hamper for everyone at the end of the course, to take to the communion picnic.

(Beat, amused) So, you're 'just here for the hamper'…

TOM   Yeah. Have you got a problem with that?

REV PHIL   *(Knowing)* No, no… God has as many different ways to reach out to his children as we have to reach out to him.

Phil looks at the next person along, nods for him to speak.

TOM	*(Won't let it lie)* Listen, God's got nothing to do with it – I'm here for the hamper and that's all I'm here for, all right?
REV PHIL	*(Slight smile)* No, right, that's fine.
TOM	Tsch. You're all the same. First off it's all, 'Oh, isn't God great'. But then the barricades start going up and soon enough it's 'let's lock ourselves in the compound and all have Phil's babies.' Right?

Off Amber's embarrassed look we:

SCENE 4

Int. Tom & Roy's flat. Eve. (Day 1).

Tom and Roy are sitting on the sofa.

ROY	*(Depressed)* You were right. That's not my world. Not any more.
TOM	So you two didn't... *(Whistles)?*
ROY	She brought Des along.
TOM	*(Sharp intake of breath)* Oooh.
ROY	They... they wanted to tell me that they're getting married.
TOM	*(Sharp intake of breath)* Ahhh.
ROY	They ordered champagne to celebrate and we split the bill.
TOM	*(Sharp intake of breath)* Shhhhh.
ROY	It was humiliating Tom.
TOM	Humiliating? Bollocks. *(Pours them both a Scotch)*

They were the ones who were humilated.
A pair of pathetic worms, suffocating in
their stupid cardigans while you sat there,
laughing away.

ROY   I wasn't laughing.

TOM   Inside. Inside you were laughing.

ROY   No I wasn't.

TOM   Anyway, we're free of all that aren't we Roy?
We're never going back to the suburban
death-hole are we Roy? No, we're a pair of
bohemians. Crazy muthahumpin' bohemians!

They clink glasses.

ROY   Heh. I suppose you're right Tom.

TOM   'Course I'm right. Go and order your coffin,
Penny, 'cos you're already dead, and while
you're nailing yourself into it, we'll be getting
high off the hog. Ah?

ROY   Ha ha!

They sip.

TOM   *(Beat)* So how about a spot of Rummicub?

*He gets out the board from under the coffee
table.*

ROY   No, no, not yet – I want to hear all about your
afternoon…

TOM   *(Groans)* Trust me, you don't.

ROY   Come on, you salty old sea dog, you can tell
me, what did you get up to, with the gorgeous
young prostitute.

TOM *(Remembering, busking)*

Oh, yes. Well, er, you know. The full monty. The whole nine yards. Brilliant.

ROY Come on. Spill the beans.

(Conspiratorial) What's it like? What's it actually physically like, with a hooker?

TOM It's like …

(Thinks) it's like putting your Walter Pidgeon in a mincing machine – of pure pleasure.

ROY *(Confused, but impressed)* Wow.

TOM *(Opening Rummicub)* Now, where are the bloody rules for this thing?

ROY It's the sort of thing we've all thought about, though, isn't it? A lovely young girl available to do your bidding. But actually doing it…

TOM *(Re. game)* Bollocks, let's just make it up as we go along, like we did with backgammon…

ROY *(Beat)* Tom, I'm thinking, here I am, a fully-functioning adult, unmarried now and probably forever, and… well… how do you fancy taking your old mate round a few of your haunts?

TOM *(Beat, uncomfortable)* Oh, uh, right, well, I don't know… I mean… you might find it a little, rich for your blood…

ROY Come on Tom, I'm a grown man. What about the little cracker you pulled this afternoon? Any more left in the box?

Off Tom's uncomfortable look we:

SCENE 5

Ext. Soho streets. Day. (Day 2).

Tom and Roy are walking down a street in Soho. Roy is excited, Tom trying to act like he does this sort of thing the whole time and knows the area well.

TOM   *(To a street trader)* Hi!

         (To a guy waiting for his girlfriend) Hello there, catch you later.

ROY   This is great isn't it Tom? It's the last days of Rome – everything's screwed, so let's screw everything!

TOM   Yep, you're with my people now Roy.

ROY   'The road of excess leads to the palace of wisdom.' That's never sounded in any way plausible, but perhaps it's true?

TOM   Of course it's true. *(Points to phone box)*

         See that? That's where Francis Bacon thought up the idea of modern art.

         (Points to lamppost) And right here me and Jeffery Bernard, we, puked in a copper's pockets. Jeff comes too, all polite, offers him three bob for his dry cleaning, the copper says, 'Mr Bernard, you puked in my pocket last Thursday'!

ROY   *(Dubious)* I didn't know you knew Jeffrey Bernard?

TOM   Well, by the end, anyone could have a go. He was like a ride at Alton Towers. Yup. Those were the days my friend!

ROY   Huh.

           (Beat, nervous, dry-mouthed) So, where do we
           go for the – girls?

TOM   Well, anywhere, old chap! Anywhere at all.
           Right here for example.

           *Looks around, motions to some dodgy stairs
           that look promising, Roy's up them in a shot,
           Tom follows.*

SCENE 6

Int. alternative health clinic. Day. (Day 2).

*Tom and Roy are upstairs in the reception at an
alternative health clinic. There is a woman in a white coat
behind a desk.*

TOM   So, reflexology is just – feet? You don't do any
           'extras'... like a quick

           (Whistles)... No?

SCENE 7

Ext. Soho street. Day. (Day 3).

*Tom and Roy are walking past an open doorway with
some 'model' type cards above the buzzers.*

TOM   I guess Sonia's moved on. We'll probably never
           know the full story. Come on, let's get a Zinger
           Tower Burger and have a laugh about it.

           Tom is moving off but Roy stays put.

ROY   *(Re: cards)* What about one of these?

(Reads) 'Katia.' She sounds nice. Exotic.

(Reaches for wallet) How much do you think she'd charge?

TOM   *(Shocked)* You're not – you're not really going to do it?

ROY   *(Adrenalized)* You know I think I really am going to do it!

TOM   *(Suddenly serious)* But – Roy, no – are you sure – 'cos – it's not – it's not, really your sort of thing is it? Come on, let's go to the park! I'll buy another aerobie, this time I promise not to throw it so hard!

ROY   *(Frowning)* You don't think I can handle it, is that it? You think I should stay where I belong, with my BBC4 and my carcoats and my cruises?

TOM   No Roy – God no – nothing like that…

ROY   Well I'm going up there Tom.

    Roy takes a deep breath and heads up the stairs.

TOM   OK, great, well. Just – take care old friend, don't – don't get hooked on it. And – you know, don't, die of ignorance. Rubber up. For goodness' sake rubber up!

A young woman walks past Roy and looks at him askance. Tom smiles back embarrassed.

SCENE 8

Int. Church Hall. Day. (Day 4).

The circle is assembling again, with Tom and Amber and Reverend Phil. A bloke sits down next to Tom.

BLOKE	*(Friendly)* I'm John.
TOM	Yeah, well I'm only here 'cos if I wasn't, there's a good chance my daughter might top herself.
	(Circles his finger at his temple as if to explain) Plus there's nothing on telly. I mean, there isn't, is there? Have you seen anything? You don't need to answer that.
REV PHIL	So, 'unconditional love.' It can be difficult to accept God's unconditional love, because we're so used to being loved conditionally.
	(Beat) Any thoughts anyone? Tom?
TOM	*(Smug)* Well, mainly I've been thinking about the four different types of cheese in the hamper.
REV PHIL	Ha ha. Good old Tom.
	(Beat) Tom, how would you feel if I said I loved you?
TOM	*(Defiant)* I'd say, try someone else, I don't bend.
	(Points to a bloke) What about him? He might be a good bet...
REV PHIL	No Tom. I'm not talking about lust. I'm talking about love. I can look you in the eye right now and tell you I love you.
TOM	*(Embarrassed)* Ha ha! He wants to bend me!

Tom looks around but no-one else is laughing.

REV PHIL   *(Intense eye contact)*

Because I can see your limitless potential for love and wisdom. The glory of what you are and can be dazzles me.

TOM   *(Uncomfortable)* Yeah, right. Whatever.

(Weakly) Bring on the hamper!

REV PHIL   If you could see yourself the way God sees you you'd never feel lonely or frightened or sick with self-hatred ever again.

TOM   *(Shifting in his seat)* Self-hatred? Me? Pull the other one. I'm great. I'm the greatest. If anything, I'm too great. My only problem is I can't handle how great I am.

REV PHIL   There's nothing but your pride standing in the way of perfect, complete happiness Tom.

(Beat) Is it that you think you're past saving?

TOM   *(Beat)* Maybe. Possibly. I'm not saying.

REV PHIL   Well you're wrong Tom. Thanks to Jesus, nobody is past saving.

TOM   *(Beat, wavering, then)* Yeah, well... tell that to Bruce Grobelaar, he's definitely past saving!

(He looks around but no-one laughs. Then, under his breath) Bollocks to you.

SCENE 9

Int. Tom & Roy's flat. Day. (Day 6).

Tom and Roy are alone in their flat. Tom is watching TV as Roy reads 'The Guardian.'

ROY   *(Re. TV)* Can you turn it down a bit?

TOM   *(Moved but hiding it)* It's just about to finish. It's a bloody good film you know. You should be watching it.

ROY   *(Frowning)* Since when were you into Jesus of Nazareth?

TOM   *(Embarassed, doesn't want to go into it)* Look, it's just a bloody good story, alright? I mean it's no Weekend at Bernie's – but, it's... funny. Anyway, just because I like chips doesn't mean I can't like... risotto. Don't box me in.

         (Beat) Anyway. I don't even like it.

         Tom, pained, switches the TV off. Looks at Roy.

TOM   *(After a beat)*

         God, do you really have to read the paper literally every day? It's so boring. You're only doing it to annoy me and it's really getting on my wick.

         (Beat, irritated, eager) Oh, for God's sakes man, come on, tell me.

ROY   What?

TOM   'What?' 'What?' he asks.

         (As if it's obvious) How was today's session with Katia?

ROY	*(Remembering rare delights)* Oh. Oh. A-mazing. Remarkable. Quite remarkable. At my age I didn't think – I just – well. It was incredible.
TOM	*(Fascinated)* Right. Right. So, what exactly do you get up to?
ROY	No. No Tom. It wouldn't be right. Sexual attraction may have been what brought us together, but our relationship's evolved into something much much more.
TOM	What?
ROY	We talk and talk you know. She understands me.
TOM	Oh Roy. Roy Roy Roy Roy Roy.
ROY	*(Defensive)* What?
TOM	Oh you ignoramus, you ingénue, you pathetic lovely little man...
ROY	Tom, the majority of couples meet in the workplace you know.
TOM	*(Sympathetic)* Come on mate. She's reeling you in like a fish. With a chemically induced erection.
ROY	I think I may have found my muse.
TOM	Your muse? Don't you have to be an artist to have a muse? You don't need a muse to do the crossword Roy.
ROY	I can have a muse if I want to.
TOM	No you can't.

ROY Listen, I'm just experiencing a little bit of happiness and excitement in my life. I don't know why that makes you so jealous.

TOM Me, jealous? Of you? That is literally a laugh. I'm laughing at that idea. Can you hear me?

    (Forces a dry little laugh) Do you hear that Roy?

ROY Hardly.

TOM Why would someone like me who has dabbled in every, flesh pot in... in the land with women of every race, creed, and council tax band be jealous of your little... fling?

ROY *(With edge)* I don't know Tom. I really don't know, actually.

TOM Yes well nor do I. Nor do I Roy.

    (Beat) So. Shut up.

SCENE 10

Int. Roy & Tom's flat. Day. (Day 8).

Amber is talking to Tom, who is flicking 'bored' through the pathway course glossy magazine.

AMBER Wasn't Phil great last night? Wasn't that a great bit of the Gospel he read out?

TOM He's a good vicar, if you like that sort of thing.

AMBER The Bible has totally become my Bible right now. I'm loving it.

TOM *(Putting down magazine)* Yeah – well it's easier for you, I'm living in Sodom and Gomorrah.

AMBER   Well I'm always saying, get a cleaner.

TOM   It's Roy. Roy's dancing to all the devil's tunes.

AMBER   Roy? Good old Roy?

TOM   Yes, 'good old Roy.' I never even see him these days. He spends all his time banging a hooker. Can you believe it? A beautiful young hooker. And what's worse, he thinks he's in love with her. He's not even torn up with guilt! It's horrible. Disgusting.

AMBER   Well, I suppose ours is not to judge. Prostitution isn't mentioned in the Ten Commandments...

TOM   Oh, right, and just because it's not covered by the Ten Commandments suddenly it's fine? I suppose it's fine to do internet fraud, lethal injections and video... gambling?

AMBER   I think you've got to take it on a case-by-case basis.

TOM   Well in this case, we've got a lonely, confused old man getting far more than his fair share. Where's my piece of pie, eh? They should make it more fun being good. I've been good all morning and I'm going out of my mind!

AMBER   Being good is its own reward in the eyes of God.

TOM   Oh God, yeah, 'God'. Who's to say this God bloke even exists anyway? I mean how are you going to feel when you've lived the most boring life imaginable only to arrive in heaven and find the whole place deserted. Answer: pretty stupid.

	(Gets up) Look, I'm going out.
AMBER	Where are you going?
TOM	*(Puts on his coat)* To have a goood time.
AMBER	Where?
TOM	*(Covering)* To... the place I go to have a good time. Laser Quest. Or paintballing.
AMBER	Laser Quest won't be open yet.
TOM	Well I'll just wait until it is. Patience is a virtue apparently, according to your best friend God.
AMBER	He's your friend too.
	(Beat, with a smile) I saw you praying in your room you know Dad.
TOM	*(On the back foot)* Praying? Me? I don't think so. No, I was just, on my knees, looking, for – something.
AMBER	What?
TOM	Oh, I don't know. That's probably why I couldn't find it. See you later!

He goes to exit.

SCENE 11

Ext. Katia's doorway – Soho. Day. (Day 11).

Tom comes down the stairs from Katia's looking satisfied, putting away his wallet, he steps into the street furtively hoping no one's seen where he's coming from.

Suddenly Roy, smartly dressed, appears, arriving with a bunch of flowers and some chocolates and a wrapped CD He is shocked to see Tom – who is equally shocked to see him.

ROY   Tom?

TOM   Roy!

     (Covering) Thought – thought I might find you round here!

ROY   Really?

TOM   Yeah. Yeah. I was looking for you. Come on, let's get down to Caesar's World, have another crack at the skiing machine, eh?

     Tom moves off, Roy doesn't follow.

ROY   But – I don't understand – I didn't tell you I'd be here…

     (Beat, hard) You've come to see Katia, haven't you?

TOM   No. What? No. Of course not. What a thing to say.

ROY   What are you doing here then? Eh?

TOM   *(Motioning to a shop)* Maybe I came down to buy some reggae LP's? Have you thought about that? No of course you haven't. Or some fruit. They do sell fruit here as well you know! It's not all just porn, hookers and amyl nitrate like you obviously think it is.

ROY   *(Eyeing Tom suspiciously)* I want you to promise me Tom, promise me that you will never try to see Katia.

TOM   You want me to promise? What about her?
                    Have you made her promise? I don't think
                    you have.

ROY   *(Uncomfortable)* That's different. It's... she
                    has her career to think about.

TOM   *(Mocking)* Her career?

ROY   *(Defiant)* Yes, her career. Now are you going
                    to promise or aren't you?

TOM   I might do. What are you going to do if I don't?

ROY   Ask you to leave my flat immediately and
                    never speak to you again.

TOM   Yes, all right, of course I promise. Lighten up.
                    I was always going to promise. I promise –
                    alright!

SCENE 12

Int. flat. Night. (Day 12).

*Tom is tidying the flat, rather excited. The doorbell rings
and he hurriedly opens the door. It's Reverend Phil.*

TOM   *(Pleased and creepy)* Phil! Phil Phil Phil Phil!
                    It's great you could make it. Thou art
                    welcome! Ha ha.

REV PHIL   *(Shakes his hand warmly)* Thanks Tom.
                    It's good to see you.

TOM   Have a seat! Sorry everything's so... crap.
                    Although, living in church, it's probably nice
                    now and again to have a soft chair.

REV PHIL   *(With a smile)* I don't actually live in church...

TOM   No, of course you don't, of course you don't, what a stupid thing to say...

                (Slaps himself hard on the head)... what an idiotic boob...

REV PHIL   Tom, it's fine, relax, sit down.

                (Beat) So, what can I do for you?

TOM   Okay – well, I've been doing a bit of reading, on what you suggested, but I've been finding it a bit weird.

REV PHIL   Oh – I hope you haven't been put off because when in the different gospels, different pictures emerge of Christ, to me that doesn't undermine his truth. It emphasises the humanity of his disciples.

TOM   *(Rapturous)* Yes! Yes. That is so shitting right.

REV PHIL   *(A bit taken aback)* Yes. Er – quite so.

TOM   And there's a burning question, an issue I've been grappling with that I was hoping you could solve.

REV PHIL   Fire away.

TOM   Yes. Right. So. There's – let's say...

                (Beat) Okay. Look, there's, this pie.

REV PHIL   Is this – a metaphorical pie?

TOM   No it's just a very very tasty pie, but the thing is, it's your friend's pie. Well it's not really his pie, he just saw it first. Although you kind of showed him where it lived. Anyway, your friend's eating the pie, and telling you how delicious it is, 'oh this is great pie, I've never had pie this good, this is literally the best pie ever, yum yum yum, everything's great since I found my lovely pie', and he's gorging himself on it and writing it letters and giving it presents night and day. In a situation like that, do you think it would it be okay to have a slice of the pie?

REV PHIL   You mean – steal some of his pie?

TOM   Didn't you hear, Phil! It's not his pie.

             (Calming) Anyway, it's a magical everlasting pie. There's plenty for everyone.

REV PHIL   I'm sorry Tom, you've lost me.

TOM   All right, all right, look – what about a friend? Can two people be friends with the same person? That's okay isn't it? That's fine? You've got to say that's fine. Right?

REV PHIL   (Non-plussed) Well – yes. Of course, I mean...

TOM   (Interrupting) Great. Brilliant. Thanks.

REV PHIL   (Beat) Is that it or was there anything else you wanted to...?

TOM   No, that's it, that's everything, everything's sorted.

REV PHIL   OK, great.

             (Goes to leave) Well it's been ...

TOM   (Interrupting, biting his lip) Actually – well – I suppose, actually I did have a more, specific question.

REV PHIL   Uh-huh.

TOM   Yes, I looked in Mark, had a hunt through the
             whole caboodle actually, it was just a point of
             interest really, about how, God, er, feels about
             the question of…

             (Quiet, almost inaudible)… prostitution.

REV PHIL   The what? Sorry I couldn't hear what…

TOM   *(Coughs)* Prostitution.

             (Phil is still blank – then, hard) Prostitution,
             all right? PROSTITUTION. Happy now?

REV PHIL   Right, I see. Prostitution – the turning of
             sexual love into a transaction?

TOM   Er, yeah, it came up in the pub quiz. I mean,
             basically is it okay for a punter, of Jesus, to
             be also a punter of, of a, a hooker?

REV PHIL   Well, I think I'd have to say no.

TOM   Right, of course, obviously. But – do you mean,
             literally, no? I mean sure, in a perfect world
             we wouldn't eat jam doughnuts, five fruit and
             veg a day etc, but in the real world… I mean,
             bottom line, Pearly Gates. Is it going to be a
             deal breaker?

REV PHIL   The important thing about any relationship,
             sexual or otherwise, is that love is present.
             If love is there then God is there also.

TOM   Right. I see. Love. 'All you need is love.'

REV PHIL   Think about it like this. Paying a woman
             for sex? How would that make you feel?
             Closer, to God? Or further away?

             Tom thinks hard, bites his lip.

TOM   Closer?

        (Phil looks at him) Is it closer? It's not closer is it?

SCENE 13

Int. Tom & Roy's flat. Eve. (Day 21).

Roy is sitting looking troubled. Tom enters whistling.

ROY   *(Accusingly but incoherently)* Ah! Ahhhh! Ah!

TOM   Are you okay mate?

ROY   You're the big friend are you?

TOM   I really have no idea what you're on about.

ROY   Recognize this?

        Roy flings Tom a sweatshirt.

TOM   Of course I recognize it. 'Arthur II: On the Rocks.' Great movie. Great sweatshirt.

ROY   And can you think perhaps where I might possibly have found that sweatshirt?

TOM   *(Non-plussed)* In my sweatshirt drawer with all my other sweatshirts?

ROY   Try again Tom.

        (Like a barrister) Try – under the bed at Katia's.

TOM   What?

        (Beat, shaken, then) Yeah, well, so what? A million people probably have this sweatshirt. Literally a million.

ROY   *(Angry)* Tom, you promised me. You promised.

TOM   It's a hugely popular film. A classic. It could be anyone's.

              (Beat) Anyway, I don't think I actually promised.

ROY   You told me, you actually said the words 'I promise'!

TOM   Oh come on Roy. Promises schromises. Have you read the Labour Party manifesto? Of course you haven't. Nobody has. They probably wrote it in an hour and a half with a bottle of schnapps and some Matchmakers.

ROY   *(Fuming)* I'm... I can't believe this Tom. I really can't believe you would do this.

TOM   Look, I am sorry Roy, I am, but really, you can't go on and on about how great Woolworths is – 'ooh, Woolworths is the best, it's amazing what you can get at Woolworths, you must go to Woolworths,' and then get all shirty when I want to go.

ROY   *(Paces, wringing hands)* So how many times have you seen her?

TOM   Not that many.

ROY   How many?

TOM   Less than ten.

ROY   Ten!?!

TOM   No, less than ten. Listen to what I say Roy.

              (Beat) More like eight.

ROY   Why Tom? For God's sake why?

THE OLD GUYS BY JESSE ARMSTRONG & SAM BAIN

TOM	Roy. Look – the first time, was a, a, a moment of madness – once and never to be repeated, but then you see – well, now, I'm in love with her. It's love.
ROY	I can't believe you'd…
TOM	And it's sort of grimly ironic I suppose because while she was playing you for the biggest rube out, she really did fall in love with me.
ROY	You have no idea… she and I… she's told me things she's never told a single soul – precious childhood stories…
TOM	Tales about her beloved Mrs Levin, the piano teacher?
ROY	*(Shocked)* She told you about Mrs Levin?
TOM	The piano teacher with all the bracelets who used to brush her hair? Yes, yes, we covered Mrs Levin in the first session.
ROY	Blimey.
	(Beat) So – you really – you love her?
TOM	Yes.
ROY	And I love her. What are we going to do?
TOM	Well I suppose the most obvious thing would be for one of us to kill ourselves.
	(Rummaging) I think I've got a coin.
ROY	Tom, we are not tossing for suicide.
	Tom's found his coin.
TOM	No?

ROY   No.

           (Beat) Especially not with your double headed
           joke shop coin.

WHAT HAPPENS NEXT?
CAN YOU HAVE THE LAST LAUGH?

Mike Davis P. I.

by Ian Brown & James Hendrie

© Mike Prince

IAN BROWN & JAMES HENDRIE

*Ian and James have been writing comedy together
since 1982. Their radio credits include: "Week
Ending", "The News Huddlines", "Saturday Night
Fry", and two series each of "Tales from the
Mausoleum Club" and "Dial 'M' for Pizza".*

*For TV they have contributed to "Red Dwarf",
"Drop the Dead Donkey", "Murder Most Horrid"
and much else. They have also written
for five series of "My Family". They live in London.
But not together.*

SCENE 1

Int. Mike's car. Day.

Mike Davis P. I. is sitting in his car, on a stake-out.

He is a slightly obsessive man in his early forties whose best years are in the past but who has an unshakeable belief in his own future.

His clothes were once 'smart casual' – now they're just 'casual'.

He speaks into mini cassette recorder and sips from a plastic cup of coffee.

MIKE   *(Into mic)* "11.35 am, Subject arrives at premises... Subject finds front door locked..." Huh... story of my life. No, don't put that bit down, Siobhan. "Subject proceeds to rear of premises..." Oh god, I wish I'd gone Chinese instead of Indian last night... don't put that down either... Ah! "11.36, front upstairs curtains drawn by Client's wife..." and the husband has no idea. Poor bastard. Out working his fingers to the bone while some pretty-boy jack-the-lad nips round and slips his kippers in the grill...

You never think it's going to happen to you. But it does. Your mind's so focussed on being "The Great Detective" that you don't notice the little tell-tale signs. Like – the smell of cigarettes in the bedroom... the strange socks in the laundry basket... the naked man in the wardrobe.

(Pause) Better leave that bit out too, Siobhan.

SCENE 2

Int. Academy Investigations office. Day.

A shabby room above a branch of "Minnesota Fried Chicken".

The antithesis of the paperless office, its shelves and part of the floor are piled with bulging files, tattered document wallets and unopened letters.

There are three desks, two of which are occupied by Mike's assistants, Francis Gammon and Siobhan Bryant.

Francis, a big, burly ex-copper in his fifties, old-fashioned in terminology and attitudes, is drinking tea and reading the local paper.

Siobhan, Mike's receptionist-cum-secretary, is in her early twenties. She is attractive, fashionable, but strictly nine-to-five. In other words, she has a life.

Siobhan is wearing headphones linked to Mike's mini cassette player, audio-typing Mike's report from last night.

Mike rushes in from the hall with a bunch of letters and a new edition of "Yellow Pages"

MIKE   It's arrived! Yellow Pages!

          Francis and Siobhan exchange a look.

          Mike tosses the letters onto a desk, rips the wrapper off the "Yellow Pages" and starts frantically leafing through.

MIKE   Let's have a look at you, my beauty!...
          Detective Agencies... Detective Agencies...
          Here we are! First in the book: "Aaacademy
          Investigations". With three "A"s. Now who
          said that was a stupid idea?

SIOBHAN	I did.
FRANCIS	I did.
MIKE	*(Re the book)* Bastards!
SIOBHAN	Excuse me?
MIKE	Someone's sneaked in before us. Bloody Brian Abbott. Or Bloody Brian Aaaabbott with four "A"s as he now appears to be called.
FRANCIS	*(Lost in admiration)* God, that's clever.
MIKE	You said it was stupid.
FRANCIS	That was with three "A"s. He's used four.
	(Marvelling) Only Brian Abbott...
	Mike starts leafing through the morning's post.
MIKE	Well, you wait till the next edition. I'll have five "A"s – no, six. No, ten. You'll see.
	(Off the letters) Oh <u>what</u>? Accident Investigation, Suspected Employee Dishonesty, Writ Serving, Accident, Accident, Writ, Writ... Runaway Rabbit... I'm fed up with these pissy little cases.
FRANCIS	That's our bread-and-butter.
MIKE	I don't want bread-and-butter. I want brioche. With Victoria plum jam. I want chocolate digestives.
FRANCIS	Oo. And a nice cup of tea.
	He takes a sip from his mug.
FRANCIS	Lovely.
MIKE	What I want is a nice, juicy murder.

Siobhan picks up the mini-cassette player and rewinds a little.

SIOBHAN   I wish you'd speak more clearly. You've got no microphone technique. It sounds like you're crying.

MIKE   I was not crying.

SIOBHAN   Well – snuffling at the very least.

MIKE   It was a runny nose. I'd had a curry. Which I think you'll find I mention in my report.

FRANCIS   Shall I tell you something interesting?

The other two ignore him.

FRANCIS   Murders are mercifully rare. In all my 20 years in the Force, I only saw two.

He pauses to let this fact sink in and takes another sip of tea.

MIKE   That's because you're lazy. Or you ran away. Or you're not very observant.

FRANCIS   Observant? I'm not the one whose wife –

Francis notes Mike's pained expression and breaks off.

FRANCIS   Nothing.

SIOBHAN   *(Breaking off typing)* Bloody hell. I wish you'd tell me which bits to leave out before you say them.

She hits the 'delete' key about 20 times.

MIKE   *(Musing)* A Serial Killer. That would be nice... Regular work... "The gift that goes on giving".

SIOBHAN	*(Still "deleting")* You disgust me. Murder's not some sort of money-spinning opportunity. Murder victims are real people with jobs and families. Normal people who work hard from nine to five.
MIKE	You'll be safe, then.
	(Then) Okay, maybe not a murder. Maybe a nice fat corruption scandal that goes Right To The Top.
SIOBHAN	You know, you'd be much happier if you didn't have these ludicrous expectations.
MIKE	They are not "ludicrous", they are "ambitious". They are not "expectations", they are "targets". And I am happy.
SIOBHAN	Not according to this tape.
	She carries on typing.
MIKE	OK – we may be on the ground floor now, but I'm going right to the top. And I'm taking you all with me.
FRANCIS	Mike – no policeman likes to hear that phrase.
	The phone rings. Siobhan answers.
SIOBHAN	Hello? Aaaaaaacademy Investigations.
	Mike dumps the "Yellow Pages" in the bin.

SCENE 3

Int. Mike's office. Later.

Siobhan breaks off from typing and heads for the door.

MIKE	Where are you off to?

SIOBHAN	Toilet.
MIKE	That's the fifth time this morning.
SIOBHAN	I've got cystitis.
MIKE	That must explain why you come back smelling of smoke.

She shrugs and exits.

Mike fiddles with the papers on his desk. something is clearly bothering him.

MIKE	So... what do you think?
FRANCIS	About what?
MIKE	You don't think I'm playing it too cool, do you?
FRANCIS	Playing what too cool?
	(A pause) Oh no! You and <u>her</u>??
MIKE	What's wrong with that?
FRANCIS	(A) She's too young for you and (B) You're too old for her. And (C) Office romances never work.
MIKE	Anything else?
FRANCIS	Oh yeah. (D) Five minutes ago she said, and I quote, "you disgust me".
MIKE	Hm, I noticed that. But maybe she had a good reason.
FRANCIS	Like – she hates you?
MIKE	Could be her time of the month.
FRANCIS	In that case it's been her time of the month every day for the last two and a half years.

MIKE   What are you saying? She hates me?

FRANCIS   Maybe hate's too strong a word. Deep resentment maybe. Or contempt. Try cutting her a bit of slack.

MIKE   What for?

FRANCIS   You really don't understand people at all, do you? To get your leg over!

Mike stares at him a beat, then:

MIKE   Yeah, you got a point.

FRANCIS   But you mind how you go, lad. I've nothing against loveless, work-based liaisons. I've had my share. But that was the seventies when sexual harassment wasn't a crime.

(With a misty look) Plus you could smoke in the office, have a pint at lunchtime, chase a bankrobber, then back to the station for tea. Good old-fashioned coppering.

MIKE   *(Now reading the paper, bored)* Go on, I'm listening.

FRANCIS   Also back then you didn't have to charge anyone before beating them up. Golden days.

The buzzer goes.

MIKE   Who's that?

FRANCIS   Your 12 o'clock. The missing person case.

MIKE   *(Rubbing hands)* I love those. "Missing person" means "person who doesn't want to be found". I could string this out till Christmas. Daily rate plus expenses.

FRANCIS   Yeah and after you've found this bloke, maybe
              you could track down your principles.

MIKE   No need. They'll be in a sack at the bottom of
              a canal. With yours.

SCENE 4

Int. Mike's office. Later.

*Mike sits at his desk opposite a new client, Ken Douglas.
He is an inoffensive little man with a sun tan.*

*Siobhan has brought her chair next to Mike's desk and is
taking notes.*

Francis is at his desk, eating a big ham salad bap.

Mike is writing on a pad.

MIKE   So Mr Douglas, how did you hear about us?

KEN   Yellow Pages.

              *Mike glances triumphantly at Francis and
              Siobhan.*

MIKE   Well, you've come to the best. Now how can
              we help you?

KEN   Well, what it is, you see –

              *Before Ken can get going, Mike holds his
              hand up.*

MIKE   Hold on.

              Mike's eyes narrow perceptively.

MIKE   Hmm. Nice tan. You've been abroad.

KEN   That's right.

MIKE   New Zealand perhaps?

We see Ken is wearing a tee-shirt reading "New Zealand".

KEN   That's amazing.

MIKE   That one's for free. Go on.

KEN   When we were kids, my brother and I were split up after our parents died and my adopted family moved to New Zealand. So I sort of lost touch with my brother.

MIKE   And you want us to find him?

KEN   Incredible. I knew you were the right man for the job.

Mike gives Siobhan a covert wink. She rolls her eyes.

MIKE   What have we got to go on?

KEN   Not a lot. I don't even know his new surname. Last I heard is he lives in this town, works as lorry driver and his name is Dave.

FRANCIS   I know a lorry driver called Dave.

MIKE   Sh.

KEN   Maybe that's him.

MIKE   Maybe it is, more likely it isn't. We can't just go for the easy option. It's our job to explore every avenue.

FRANCIS   I could ring him now if you like.

Mike springs to his feet, cutting Francis off.

MIKE   Well, we won't take up any more of your time.

             (Guiding him towards the door) You've given us plenty to work on but don't expect miracles.

	It may be well after Christmas before you hear anything.

Francis shakes his head sadly.

KEN	Oh, that's no good.
FRANCIS	That's what I said.
KEN	I need results. Quickly. Tell you what, you find my brother within the week, and I'll pay you a thousand pounds.
MIKE	Well, that would be a breach of my principles but, you know –
FRANCIS	– they're at the bottom of a canal.
KEN	Pardon?
MIKE	Siobhan. Show Mr Douglas out, please.
SIOBHAN	Why?
MIKE	*(Losing it slightly)* Because it's your flipping job.

She throws her pad down on the desk and ill-naturedly shows Ken Douglas out.

SIOBHAN	Uhn. "Do this, do that".
	(To Ken) Come on, you.

She and Ken exit.

FRANCIS	And that was cutting her slack, was it?
MIKE	I said "please" didn't I?
	(Off Francis's look) Well, what do you suggest?
FRANCIS	I dunno, you could let her go home early some days.

MIKE	If she goes home any earlier, she'll be leaving before she arrives.
FRANCIS	Technically that's impossible.
	Pause
MIKE	Where is she, by the way?
FRANCIS	Gone for an early lunch.
MIKE	How do you work that out?
FRANCIS	She took her coat and her handbag.
MIKE	Huh?
FRANCIS	Didn't spot that, did you? Good old-fashioned coppering, that was.
MIKE	Oh, piss off.
FRANCIS	Ta, Mike. Back in an hour. Make it an hour and a half.
MIKE	You've <u>had</u> your lunch.
FRANCIS	That was a mid-morning bap.
	Francis exits.

SCENE 5

Int. Mike's office. Later.

Mike is eating a sandwich at his desk.

An old woman comes through the door. She's wearing a shawl and leans heavily on a stick.

NEVILLE	Hello, dearie. Buy me lucky heather?
MIKE	*(Wearily)* Hello, Neville.

The old woman straightens up and speaks with a man's voice, a booming theatrical baritone. It is Neville St. Clair, an ageing actor.

NEVILLE   Damn. You've penetrated my mufti. It's the wig, isn't it? I'll have a word with wardrobe.

MIKE   I keep telling you, Neville. You don't have to try so hard.

NEVILLE   If I didn't try so hard, I wouldn't be me.

MIKE   We can but hope. The idea is you blend into the background. That way they don't see you coming till you've served the writ. At the moment you look like you're in the chorus of "Mary Poppins".

NEVILLE   Where do you think I got the costume? So what do you have for me?

MIKE   The usual. A couple of divorce papers. A writ. A summons or two.

Mike tosses him a bundle of documents

NEVILLE   Hm, looks a bit work-a-day. Haven't you got something where I can really shine? I could use "Major Dalloway". Toothbrush moustache, ramrod back, full uniform...

(With relish)... and a monocle.

MIKE   I'll bear it in mind.

NEVILLE   Bless you.

On his way out, Neville passes Siobhan as she enters.

NEVILLE	*(To Siobhan, as old lady)* Tatty-bye, dearie.
	He exits.
SIOBHAN	Who was that?
MIKE	Oh, that's just... an old lady I'm kind to on a regular basis.
SIOBHAN	So you have to be old, do you?
	She starts taking her coat off.
MIKE	Here, listen, Siobhan – why don't you knock off early today?
SIOBHAN	O.K. Bye.
	Siobhan pulls her coat back on and exits quickly, passing Francis as he enters.
FRANCIS	<u>She's</u> in a hurry. So you asked her out.
	He starts taking his coat off.
MIKE	I said she could go home early.
FRANCIS	Oh. In that case, I wonder if I...
	He starts pulling his coat back on.
MIKE	No. Sit down, we've got work to do.
	Francis keeps his coat on and remains standing. He shifts uneasily, something on his mind.
FRANCIS	Um, Mike? There's something I've been meaning to ask you.
MIKE	I'm flattered but you said office romances don't work.
	Francis laughs nervously at this "joke".

FRANCIS	No, what it is, you see... Would it upset you awfully if I wasn't here?
MIKE	<u>Upset</u>!? Does this look upset?
	(Punching the air) Wa-hey!! Yay!! Yippee!! Hurray!
FRANCIS	Only I've been headhunted.
MIKE	*(Pleased with himself)* <u>You</u>? Who'd want to headhunt <u>you</u>? Someone looking for a fat head.
	Mike chuckles.
FRANCIS	Brian Abbott.
	Mike stops chuckling.
MIKE	What?
FRANCIS	I'm going to work for Brian Abbott.
MIKE	You...? I don't know what to say.
FRANCIS	What about "Good luck, well done, and I wish you all the best for the future"?
MIKE	What about "You bastard! You disloyal treacherous bastard!'"? When did this happen?
FRANCIS	About six weeks ago.
MIKE	You mean, I've been harbouring a viper in my bosom for six weeks? Why didn't you tell me before?
FRANCIS	Because I knew you'd take it like this.
MIKE	Like what, you bastard!
	(Then) Give me one good reason why you're leaving.

FRANCIS	He's paying me more.
	(Beat)
MIKE	Give me another reason.
FRANCIS	You don't treat me very well.
MIKE	*(Nonplussed)* Wha– all right, forget it. You might as well just... bugger off.

Francis gets up to leave.

MIKE	Hey – where are you going?
FRANCIS	You just told me to –
MIKE	You can bloody well work your month's notice.
FRANCIS	Are you serious?
MIKE	Yes.
FRANCIS	OK.

Francis sits at his desk.

FRANCIS	So what do you want me to do?
MIKE	Nothing. I'm not letting you feast your greedy little eyes on my sensitive documents. You'll only go leaking it to Brian Bloody Abbott. In fact, that's the only possible reason he hired you in the first place. Mark my words – he'll pump you for information about my business then cast you aside like a screwed-up Kleenex. In a teenager's bedroom.

Mike grabs the papers from off Francis's desk and yanks out Francis's modem cable.

Mike returns to his desk and starts feverishly writing up case notes.

> *Francis sits at his empty desk, drumming his fingers.*
>
> *(Pause)*

FRANCIS   Mike –

MIKE   *(Silencing him)* Kleenex.

SCENE 6

Int. the office kitchenette. Next day.

The kitchenette is a long, thin room with a sink, worktop, fridge, kettle & microwave.

Mike, sleeve rolled up, is attaching a radio mic to his arm. Siobhan is examining an earpiece wired to a mini cassette recorder.

MIKE   Right. What I'm going to do is to get Mr Dennehy to admit on tape that he's selling dodgy M.O.T. certificates. Got that?

SIOBHAN   Duh!

She puts the earpiece in.

MIKE   Okay. Can you hear me?

SIOBHAN   Of course I can hear you. I'm standing right next to you.

MIKE   Well, stick your finger in your other ear and listen through the earpiece.

SIOBHAN   With <u>these</u> nails? Why don't I just go back in the office?

MIKE   Because the office is no longer secure. At least while Big Ears is still working for me.

SIOBHAN   Then why don't you sack him?

MIKE	Because that's what he wants me to do.
SIOBHAN	*(Scornfully)* That's so sad.
MIKE	Just put your hand over your ear.
	Siobhan puts her hand over her ear and switches on the tape.
MIKE	This is a test recording for the "Dennehy Case". Hello Siobhan: one, two, one, two – can you hear me?
SIOBHAN	Yes. I can.
MIKE	So Siobhan – testing testing – What sort of things do you like to do in the evenings?
SIOBHAN	Clubs, movies, dancing. Depends.
MIKE	Uh-huh. Siobhan – testing, testing – perhaps one night you'd like to go to movies, clubs or dancing with... me! – testing, testing.
	Siobhan enters into the spirit of things and laughs disdainfully.
SIOBHAN	<u>You</u>? You must be joking!
MIKE	Haha – testing testing.
SIOBHAN	It'd be like going out with my granddad.
MIKE	Haha! Testing!
SIOBHAN	Plus I find you a bit too creepy.
MIKE	Ah... Well, that was fun, wasn't it? Equipment seems to be working fine. I'll er – see you down there.
	Mike walks out of the kitchenette, stunned.

SCENE 7

Int. Mike's office. (continuous).

Mike wanders in. Francis is sitting at his empty desk staring into space.

MIKE   Um, Francis. Do you find me creepy?

FRANCIS   I might do... Or I might not. I'm not saying.
            People might think I'm a blabbermouth who
            tells everybody's secrets.

MIKE   Just – just – get on with – not doing anything.

            Mike exits.

SCENE 8

Int. a café. day.

Mike is at a table with Mr Dennehy, a dodgy car dealer.

Sitting at a table far in the background, out of earshot, is Siobhan having an "innocent" cup of tea. In reality she is listening to their conversation over her earpiece.

MIKE   So, let me get this straight. You have the
            blank forms already stamped and signed
            by the garage.

MR DENNEHY Yes! I've already told you three times. Are you
            deaf or something?

MIKE   No I –

MR DENNEHY Do you want these certificates or not?

MIKE   Yes, I just want to make sure. *(Glances
            towards Siobhan)*

MR DENNEHY Well, while you're deciding I'm off for a slash.

Mr Dennehy leaves the table. Mike casts another look at Siobhan.

MIKE   *(Talking quietly into his sleeve)* Siobhan, if you got that, give me a sign.

Across the room Siobhan throws up her hands in a triumphant double thumbs-up.

MIKE   *(Quietly)* Steady!

Suddenly another man (Bob) appears.

BOB   Hi Mike! How you doing?

MIKE   Hello, mate. Um, I'm a bit busy at the moment.

Bob sits in Mr Dennehy's chair.

BOB   Not got time to chat?

MIKE   Actually it's a bit awkward...

BOB   How's that girl? What's her name – Siobhan?

MIKE   *(Aware that Siobhan is listening)* Fine, fine. Very efficient. As ever!

BOB   You got off with her yet?

MIKE   I don't know what you mean.

BOB   Come on! You've been trying to get into her knickers for months.

MIKE   You must be thinking of someone else.

BOB   No. It's definitely Siobhan. The one with the arse on her.

MIKE   *(Nodding towards the counter)* I think your tea's ready.

BOB He'll bring it over. Have her spots cleared up?

In the background we see Siobhan jump to her feet, charge over and slap Mike's face.

The whole café, including Mr Dennehy, who has just emerged from the toilet, stare at Mike askance.

SCENE 9

Int. Mike's office. Day.

Siobhan is typing angrily, pounding away at the keyboard.

Francis is at his desk, building an elaborate house of cards.

Mike walks in sheepishly with a teapot and a mug.

MIKE Cup of tea, anyone?

FRANCIS *(Perking up)* Oo.

MIKE Not you, Francis. Siobhan? Cup of tea?

Siobhan pounds the keyboard harder.

MIKE *(Trying a new tack)* Okay. Ken Douglas's missing brother. Any leads?

Silence.

MIKE Siobhan – you were ringing round all the local haulage firms.

More silence.

MIKE Francis, you –

FRANCIS – don't work here any more. Remember?

MIKE "Don't work here any more..."

(Then) I'll tell you what, Siobhan. If we can make a clean start and you forget what the bloke in the café said – who's a notorious liar anyway – then I'll give you a nice pay rise. Starting next month.

FRANCIS He can't <u>afford</u> a pay rise.

MIKE *(Gesturing him to shut up)* Ch– ch–

FRANCIS He's promising things he can't deliver. Just to get you back on side.

MIKE Don't <u>tell</u> her!

SIOBHAN Ha! I see.

MIKE *(Sotto; to Francis)* Blabbermouth!

FRANCIS Look, for your information, I didn't tell Brian Abbott anything. Apart from your idea to put 3 A's in "Academy Investigations".

Mike slowly turns to look at Francis.

SCENE 10

Ext. street. Moments later.

Francis stumbles out of the door to "Academy Investigations".

A beat later, his coat is thrown out after him.

The door slams shut.

SCENE 11

Int. Mike's car. Day.

Mike and Siobhan are sitting in Mike's car, parked outside a house. Mike has a camera.

Siobhan is still in a huff.

SIOBHAN   You can't just buy people off, you know.

MIKE   So you don't want the pay rise.

SIOBHAN   I'm not saying that. I'm saying it's not just about money. People have feelings, and I'm still angry.

MIKE   All right. I'll raise it another twenty quid. Feeling better?

SIOBHAN   Much.

MIKE   Good. Now we can get on with waiting for Ken Douglas's brother to show up.

SIOBHAN   I don't understand. Why all the cloak and dagger stuff?

MIKE   Because we have to be discreet. How would you feel if your long-lost brother suddenly popped up wanting to see you?

SIOBHAN   I haven't got a long-lost brother.

MIKE   But suppose that you did.

SIOBHAN   I'm not that imaginative.

MIKE   Oh. In that case. How would you like to go to a hotel bar with me and, you know, discuss the case?

SIOBHAN   Yeah, okay.

Mike is chuffed. In his wing mirror he sees a big flash Mercedes approaching.

MIKE Ah, there we go. That's the car I want...
CLK Kompressor, alloy wheels, V-12 bi-turbo
engine, 0-60 in 4 seconds. I just need to solve
the Big One, get my name in the paper.
Won't be for a couple of years mind.

*The Mercedes pulls alongside and peeps its
horn.*

*We see that the driver is Francis, who gives a
big smile and a wave. He parks a couple of
cars in front of Mike's.*

MIKE Bastard! Bloody Brian Abbott.

(Then) Anyway, they're not that great. Took
one for a test drive, once. Really tinny and
they're famous for the bad suspension...

*Mike turns to Siobhan who has got out of the
car.*

MIKE Hey – where are you going?

SIOBHAN Thought I'd sit in Francis's car. Looks comfier.

(Then, realising) Hang on a minute –
"Hotel Bar"?

She slams the door and stomps off.

SCENE 12

Int. the café. Day.

*Mike leaves the counter with his cup of tea, looking for
somewhere to sit.*

*He spots Francis sitting at a table, obviously having a
meeting with an army major.*

Francis's clothes are noticeably smarter than when he worked for Mike.

MIKE   Hey – what are you doing here?

FRANCIS   Hello Mike, how's things?

MIKE   You can't use this café, this is our café.

FRANCIS   <u>Your</u> café?

MIKE   Academy Investigations. We've always used it. Kindly conduct your business elsewhere.

FRANCIS   It's not like you own it. You can hardly pay the rent on your office.

MIKE   How do you know?

FRANCIS   Brian Abbott told me.

Mike is stunned.

FRANCIS   Come on, Mike. Sit down. No hard feelings, eh?

Mike sits down reluctantly.

FRANCIS   How's business? Made any progress with the Ken Douglas thing?

MIKE   *(With bravado)* Oh yeah. Pretty much in the bag. Found the brother. Even got a photo of – Hey! I know your game. Pinching my trade secrets.

Mike double-takes as he looks at the major's face. He leans in to get a closer look. Then leans in even further.

MIKE   Neville?

NEVILLE   *(For it is he)*

	Major Dalloway, if you don't mind.
FRANCIS	Good costume, isn't it, Mike? He's doing a bit of process-serving for me.
MIKE	So you're not only using my café you're using my, my – what are you, Neville?
NEVILLE	A Master of Disguise.
MIKE	Whatever. <u>I</u> get first dibs on Neville. I found him, I trained him, I pay his fines. And I need him for a vital job that must take priority.
NEVILLE	O.K. But I'm not allowed within 2 miles of the town centre.
MIKE	What?
NEVILLE	Under the terms of my ASBO.
MIKE	ASBO? Isn't that for young lads?
NEVILLE	In a manner of speaking, it is.
	(Then) So what's this vital job? Sounds thrilling.
MIKE	I want you to buy Siobhan some flowers. Normally I'd ask her to do it but it doesn't seem appropriate.

Francis rolls his eyes.

SCENE 13

Int. Mike's office. Day.

There is a big vase of lovely flowers on Siobhan's desk.

Siobhan finally looks happy for a change. She is typing brightly.

Ken Douglas sits before Mike's desk. Mike is handing him an envelope.

MIKE   There you go, Mr Douglas. Name, address, workplace – there's even a photograph.

KEN   That's marvellous. You don't know how much this means to me. And he has no idea I'm looking for him?

MIKE   None whatsoever.

KEN   Oh good. I can't wait to see the expression on his face when he sees me. Heh heh.

WHAT HAPPENS NEXT?
CAN YOU HAVE THE LAST LAUGH?

Love for Sale

by Jonathan Harvey

© 6th Floor

JONATHAN HARVEY

Jonathan comes from Liverpool and is the proud parent of 16 plays, several television series and a coming out movie. He has won several major awards for his writing, and also the Space Hopper Championships at Butlins, Pwhelli.

He has worked extensively in television, on shows as diverse as Coronation Street, Big Brother and At Home With The Braithwaites. He created the BAFTA nominated sitcom Gimme Gimme Gimme, but his proudest moment was when his film Beautiful Thing won 'Best Gay Film Ever' on Gay.com. His sexuality influences his writing, and his moods influence his stunning dress sense.

SCENE 1

Int. lounge: day.

Bo sits at her table, plucking hairs out of her chin, an alice band scraping her hair back as she continues to make herself up. Roy, Matt and Vinnie lounge around on the sofa. Vinnie is reading a book and smoking a cigarette. Matt is flicking between television channels with the remote. Roy is miming driving a car.

ROY	D'you know what I could eat now?
VINNIE	What?
ROY	Pizza.
	They sit there.
ROY	Thin 'n' crispy. American hot. With extra chilli.
VINNIE	*(To Matt)* Where did you get to yesterday?
ROY	Dough balls.
MATT	*(To Vinnie)* Family funeral.
ROY	Mozarelli and tomato salad.
VINNIE	I hate funerals.
ROY	Death by Chocolate.
BO	*(Bo sniffs up)* I can smell cabbage.
	They all sniff up. Roy loses concentration on his 'driving' and has to struggle to regain control of the 'car'. Vinnie eyes him suspiciously.
MATT	The vicar had a glass eye.
VINNIE	You're joking!

BO	*(Still on about the cabbage)* It's seeping through the whole bungalow.
MATT	It fell out in the middle of 'The Wheels On The Bus'.
BO	It'll impregnate me soft furnishings.
VINNIE	Funny choice for a funeral.
BO	'What is that heavenly scent you're wearing Bo Jangles?'
MATT	She was always unconventional.
BO	'Eau de Bubble 'N' Squeak, darl!'
MATT	First funeral I've been to on ice.
BO	I went to a family funeral once. The whole family laid out by the altar. Gran on the left. Graduating coffins down to little toddler on the right. Ah, so sweet! I think they'd perished in a house fire. I know it was a No Smoking wake.
VINNIE	Were you close to them?
BO	It was so long ago... I guess I must have been on about Row G?
VINNIE	No, were you like...
BO	Oh right. No. Didn't know them from Adam. I was on a motoring tour of Okatawa at the time, which as you know, is renowned for its murderous rainfall. I'd just nipped in to stop my perm from tightening. Anyway, I'm just unfurling my one-size-fits-all pixie style rain hood when they start rollin' 'em in! And once they start, they just don't stop. Jees, it was like the bloody Generation Game. Six coffins and a cuddly toy.

VINNIE	*(To Matt)* So which member of your family was it?
ROY	Their Claire.
MATT	My cousin.
ROY	Ah. She died falling down the stairs, tripping over her own flares, whilst choking on a pear. Ah, she'da been proud o'me then. She was a poet.
BO	I think that's the way I'd like to go. Peacefully.
ROY	Sorry. *He mimes parking the car.*
ROY	I find it really difficult to drive and have a conversation.
VINNIE	Did you know her like?
ROY	Who?
VINNIE	Matt's cousin.
ROY	Their Claire? I went to one of her creative writing courses, couple o'years back. Thought I had a book in me.
VINNIE	And did you?
ROY	It was more of a pamphlet.
BO	I started a book once. 'Josie and her Amazing Yet Beguiling Prolapsed Womb'.
VINNIE	Did it not have legs?
BO	About the only thing it didn't have.
ROY	*(Roy looks to Vinnie)* Why d'you hate funerals? Do they really mess with your head?

VINNIE	No, I just hate going anywhere where you can't wear trainers.
BO	Did I tell you that my little Carmel's got back with Tin-Tin?
MATT	No.
ROY	They've had a spate of tragic deaths in Matt's family, haven't you Matt? Last year his cousin Colin was doing a sponsored parachute jump for Kids In Crisis.
VINNIE	Oh he didn't land on a couple did he?
MATT	No!
BO	He's had her initials tattooed on his upper lip. Though as her name is Carmel Urusula Nina Thomas it's rather unfortunate. Still, if I'm not very much mistaken I think we'll soon be hearing the little patter of wedding bells.
ROY	Was it Kids In Crisis?
MATT	Yeah.
BO	I've not slept for a week. I've been popping the Nytol like nobody's business.
ROY	Or was it Kids In Crumpsall?
MATT	Crisis. Kids In Crisis, it's a charity.
BO	Oh I'll always put my hand in my pocket for young kids.
VINNIE	I've heard Michael Jackson says the self same thing.
ROY	Only his thingy didn't open did it?

MATT	That's right Roy. They said at the inquest. That was the exact same words the coroner used.
ROY	Don't take the piss!
MATT	'M'lord? His thingy didn't open.'
BO	Was it suicide do you think?
MATT	I don't think so. He'd set the video to record Popstars: The Rivals, so...
BO	God, things were bad. My Andantino tried to top himself, summer of '83. But it was more a cry for help. Otherwise why throw yourself out of a ground floor window?
ROY	*(To Vinnie)* Have you ever seen a dead body?
	Vinnie nods his head.
BO	Oh I've seen heaps.
ROY	In the concentration camps?
BO	Roy! How many times do I have to tell you? I am only thirty eight and a very small half.
VINNIE	When me Dad died, me Ma dragged me in the front parlour to see him laid out. She goes, 'Take a good look. Get used to death. One of these days it might be someone you're close to'.
ROY	Did he look at peace?
VINNIE	Hard to tell behind a Freddie Kruger mask.
BO	*(Bo suddenly screams at the phone)* Ring!!

Roy is looking stunned. Vinnie rolls his eyes.

VINNIE   He looked fine. I spat on his knuckle duster. Give it a bit of a buff.

ROY   Ooh I could just go for a nice slice o'pizza.

BO   I would say. In my huge history of prostitution in hemispheres both North and South. I have had punters die on me, whoo, about eighteen times?

ROY   Does it freak you out?

BO   No it pisses me off. Well you don't bloody well get paid! What are we in it for?

ROY/MATT/   *(Half heartedly)* The money!
VINNIE

BO   Yeah! And we are gonna earn a small fortune today. I can feel it in me waters!

Just then her phone starts to ring.

BO   See? What did I tell you? I'm psychic! Things are looking up!

BO   *(She answers)* Good morning, Love For Sale, Bo speaking, how can I help? Well Sir you have come to the right place. Today on duty we have three fresh faced college jock types who are hot, horny, and ready to roll. First up we have baby faced Roy, who loves to be bad, but don't let that naïve grimace put you off. He's hung like a pony and goes like a horse.

Roy crosses his legs uncomfortably.

BO	Next up we have Matt. Matt is Eton educated and a stunning English rose.
	Roy and Vinnie look at Matt, incredulous.
BO	I'll let you into a little secret, caller. Matt's a virgin. But he's ready to try anything with the right guy, and you sound like you might be right up his alley. Possibly within the next half an hour. And finally there's Vinnie. Vinnie's a rugged ex-pro footballer with a lot more than dribbling on his mind. He's lean, he's mean and straight as a dye. Is that a rolling pin in his pocket or..
	Vinnie rolls his eyes.
BO	Sorry? Well that's not very nice is it?
BO	*(She puts the phone down)* I think it was those Christians again.
ROY	Why what did they say?
BO	He hopes we all catch AIDS and die.
	She starts filing her nails. Just then there is a knock at the door.
BO	Fuck, what if it's him?
VINNIE	You haven't ordered a pizza have you?
ROY	Not yet no.
MATT	D'you want me to get it?
	Bo is putting her glasses on and inspecting the CCTV.
BO	No. I'm made of stronger stuff than that boys. Whoever it is has got some sort of disguise on. Why do they do that? Come on, it's bound to

be a punter. Primp yourselves. Our next fifty bucks just darkened the dado.

She leaves. They all sit up and await being called through. Roy passes round some chewing gum.

ROY   Does anyone want any chewy?

They all chew.

ROY   I hope it's not that bloke with the briefcase again. He likes me to pretend to be Gordon Brown.

(He dials a number on the phone) Was Gordon Brown one of the Mister Men?

MATT   Yes.

VINNIE   Who you ringing?

ROY   Pizza.

VINNIE   But what if it's a punter, y'knob?!

ROY   Well then I've got summat nice to look forward to at the end of it.

Bo returns with Carmel, who is wearing a veil.

BO   Panic over, look who it isn't.

CARMEL   Hiya lads, it's only Carmel. Ah did you think you were gonna earn some dosh?

ROY   I'm just glad it's not that bloke with the briefcase.

(On phone please) Hiya can I order a delivery please?

BO   If you don't mind me saying, darl. You seem to be wearing a net curtain on your barnet. New look?

CARMEL   Oh Dad it's a veil int it?

BO   Oh right, so...

CARMEL   I'm doing a test run of it to see if a) it suits
            b) it's comfy and c,d and e, really.

BO   It makes you look a bit like Pam Ferris circa
            Rosemary and Thyme, and I'm not sure that's
            the best look for retail therapy.

CARMEL   Dad. Sit down. I've got some important news.

ROY   One American hot, extra chilli, dough balls
            and Death by Chocolate.

            Bo sits.

CARMEL   Last night, Dad, Tin-Tin took me up
            The Backy.

BO   Too much information, darl!

CARMEL   The field round the back of our mock Tudor
            living ambience! And you'll never guess what
            happened!

ROY   42 Melody Crescent. Roy. Thanks. *(Phone
            down)*

BO   What?! What?!

ROY   Our Janetty-Anne got molested down that
            Backy. By a fella in a monkey mask.

VINNIE   Is she devastated?

ROY   God yeah. She can only watch Planet of the
            Apes through a raffia blind.

CARMEL   *(Snaps)* I'm talking!!!

            They all look at her.

	Anyway. He got down on bended knee. Looked me right in the eye.
VINNIE	Christ he must have a long neck. What is he, a giraffe?
BO	Vinnie, do you mind? My daughter is breaking some news.
MATT	Sure she's not breaking wind? Something stinks.
BO	It's next door's bloody cabbage! *(Screaming to wall)*
	I'm trying to run a brothel in here!!
	(Calming) Sorry Carmel. You were saying.
CARMEL	Anyway, he said 'Carmel Ursula Nina Thomas. Oh spume on my ebbing tide of life.'
ROY	Is that rude?
BO	No it's poetry!
VINNIE	You should know, you've done a course.
BO	Shut up!
CARMEL	'Will you do me the honour. Of becoming. My bitch.'
BO	Oh that is so romantic. Isn't that romantic? I think this calls for a celebratory glass of vino. Matt? Grab us a bottle out of the fridge. And make sure it's not the Poppers, we've got to raise a toast!
	(To Carmel) So you're just test driving the veil. You are such a forward planner Carmel, you think of everything.

Matt goes in the fridge and gets some glasses and bottle of cheap bubbly out.

CARMEL   I'm not sure I like this one. I were getting some right funny looks on the bus.

BO   It's not what you could call a slimming veil. It'd look great on an anorexic, coz I think it makes you look fatter.

MATT   If that's possible.

CARMEL   I've got the burka effect one reserved next.

BO   Oh that sounds an interesting proposition Carmel.

CARMEL   According to Barbara in the bridal hire shop they're dead popular.

BO   What a blast, eh?

ROY   Have you decided where you're getting married?

CARMEL   I'm looking into St. Ivel's on the High Street.

BO   Oh that's a beautiful church. And that lovely lady priest. With the facial hair problem. I think it's great when your vicar actually looks like Jesus, no matter what sex they are.

CARMEL   Oh Dad, you don't think the burka effect veil'll be too offensive to that vicar? Didn't you say she was a Libyan?

BO   Lesbian, darl.

CARMEL   I wondered why her fella were called Maureen.

ROY   I grew up opposite a flat full of lesbians.

VINNIE   Dunlickin'?

ROY   One of them had a sticker in her car. 'If you
              can read this, thank a teacher'.

MATT   And did you?

ROY   Did I what?

MATT   Did... nothing.

CARMEL   Dad I was wondering if I could borrow your
              laptop to go online and investigate posies.

BO   Help yourself darl. You might have to blow the
              cobwebs off my mouse though, it's been that
              long since I clicked.

              *Carmel sits at Bo's computer and starts typing
              away. Bo watches proudly over her shoulder.*

BO   I suppose this means I'm gonna get a phone
              call from your mother. I better phone ahead
              and check what she's wearing. Wouldn't want
              to clash. Like last time. You wouldn't think
              there'd be too many parakeet yellow puffballs
              with matching pillar-box beret and fingerless
              mitts knocking about Wilmslow, but how
              wrong can you be? Oh Matt you're an angel.

              Matt has poured everyone a glass of bubbly.

VINNIE   An Eton educated angel, no less.

BO   Cheers queers!

              They all raise their glasses.

ROY   D'you think I should phone back the pizza
              place and say it's the redhead I want to
              deliver me bits?

MATT   If you want to make a complete and utter twat
          of yourself, yes.

BO   Oh don't be mean spirited Matt. Surely you
          remember what it was like to have a crush on
          someone before you hooked up with Sharon-
          Louise.

MATT   Madonna. When she did the Vogue video.
          I didn't even have to touch myself and...

VINNIE   And you reckon you're not gay?

ROY   I had a spontaneous omission over Mike
          Baldwin once.

          They survey him oddly.

ROY   He were bending over to mend the wonky
          pedal on an Underworld Singer, and... blimey
          them slacks were tight!

BO   That veil is actually giving you a rash Carmel.
          I think you should de-net.

CARMEL   Oh no I got that off Tin-Tin when he last
          slapped me. Doctor Pardeep said it were
          impetiginous.

BO   No mean feat with a Hydrobad accent.

CARMEL   However the veil does feel to be welding itself
          onto my weeping square, so maybe you're
          right. *She takes her veil off.*

MATT   Your Tin-Tin knocks you about?

BO   No he's stopped doing that. He went on a
          course didn't he?

CARMEL   Intermediate Tap Dancing. Anger
              management were full. But now, if he feels the
              need to slap someone, he just does a step ball
              change.

VINNIE   But he's obviously hit you recently.

CARMEL   No we've taken up kick boxing. Only he
              sprained his ankle on a protruding flag so
              we kind of improvise.

BO   You should write to the council.

CARMEL   I doubt they'd be that fussed really. I wrote
              to them when I missed that period and never
              heard a dickie.

              They all take this in.

CARMEL   Oh Matt, I meant to say. I were dead sorry to
              hear about your loss.

ROY   *(Gasps)* What have you lost?

BO   The death in his family!

VINNIE   Prick.

CARMEL   *(To Matt)* Your Claire.

MATT   Our Claire.

ROY   *(To Vinnie)* I thought it was their Claire.

MATT   No probs Carmel.

CARMEL   I saw her obituary in the Evening News.

ROY   Ah, wannit lovely Carm?

CARMEL   It's the first time I've seen one done in the
              style of a limerick.

BO	This wine's not very cold is it Matt? You wouldn't be a doll and get some cubes out of me ice box?
ROY	Some snacks'd be nice. Just to tide me over til the pizza gets here.
BO	Have a root around in the larder darl.
	Matt and Roy rummage around in the kitchen.
VINNIE	How can you eat so much and stay so thin? I wish I was like that.
ROY	Well I'm still young aren't I?
VINNIE	I've just gotta walk past a sweet shop and I'm bursting out me clothes like The Incredible Hulk.
ROY	And you're like... really old.
BO	So. D'you think this means you might get to meet Tin-Tin's family?
CARMEL	It's in the balance whether he invites his Mum or not, wedding-wise. She's got a nasty habit of publicly pleasuring herself. Which won't look too good on the snaps.
BO	Has she still not been treated for that? Oh the poor thing, she should see a sex therapist, they could cure that with a click of the fingers.
VINNIE	*(Vinnie nods)* In a snatch.
	Carmel clicks away at the computer. Vinnie lights another cigarette. Matt puts some ice into a bucket while Roy arranges some biscuits on a plate.
VINNIE	D'you remember the Incredible Hulk?

Matt nods.

VINNIE   They brought him back didn't they?

MATT   Well he was incredible, wasn't he?

VINNIE   I wish they'd bring Paddington back.

BO   Poor Tin-Tin. No-one likes to think of a parent
           having desires.

MATT   No, all the human beings in that used to freak
           me out.

VINNIE   Did they?

BO   I remember walking in on Mother with the
           curtains drawn and Patrick Swayze frozen on
           her box. The remnants of a sausage dinner
           scattered around her tumpty. We played Dirty
           Dancing at her send-off.

ROY   I didn't know your mam were dead.

CARMEL   No she moved to Poole.

BO   I said 'What's Poole got to offer that you can't
           get in Prenton?' She just laughed and said
           'Watersports, Brian' and buggered off.

MATT   *(Matt comes over with some ice)* Here you go.
           Roy's bringing up the rear with some chocolate
           fingers.

VINNIE   The Soup Dragon used to freak me out. And
           the Clangers.

MATT   Yeah but the human beings in Paddington
           weren't even 3-D.

VINNIE   True.

ROY   Telly freaks me out full stop. I mean when you really think about it it's weird int it? A box in the corner of the room. With folk in it. Talking. God I'm freaking myself out just thinking about it. Someone change the subject!

VINNIE   I wouldn't worry about not meeting Tin-Tin's ma, y'know Carm. I reckon parents are over-rated.

BO   Oh, thanks!

VINNIE   I look at me ma now and just think. 'What have we got in common?'

ROY   Bad skin?

VINNIE   *(Menacingly, to Roy)* And the propensity to slap twats when they're giving lip!

ROY   Eh?

MATT   *(To Vinnie)* You'll have to take up tap dancing.

ROY   I know what you mean though Vinnie. I woke up one morning. Looked at me mam and dad and thought. 'Jesus. It's like you've evolutionised into a new species. The pair o'you. It's like I don't even know you.'

             They all nod sagely. It's unusual for him to be so deep.

ROY   And I didn't. Coz I'd woke up in the orang-utan pen at Chester Zoo.

             They all sit there thinking. Bo sniffs up.

ROY   Been on a bit of a bender. I was mortified.

BO   Can you sue neighbours over cabbage style aromas?

ROY	It was nice in that pen. I stayed the whole week.
VINNIE	*(To Bo)* You could but you'll get your tyres slashed. She's vicious, her.
ROY	Aren't orangutan's lovely?
BO	Not on my Vauxhall Clitoris!
CARMEL	Renault Clio!
BO	You're such a killjoy Carmel! Honestly. Sometimes it's a wonder that I ever gave birth to you.
CARMEL	You didn't Dad! You just provided the sperm.
BO	Language Carmel! Of course I know I didn't. I'm not a complete imbicile. Though I did dream I was pregnant the other night. After one too many Dairyleas during Question Time.
MATT	Do you watch Question Time?
BO	I never miss it!
VINNIE	I didn't have you down as political Bo.
BO	Oh I'm not. I'm just a sucker for an outsize oval table. They've got a humdinger of a one that I'd love for my lounge diner, so I watch it week in week out to see if it's mentioned in the credits. But they go by that quick. Talk about lickerty split.
VINNIE	I love a good political debate.
BO	I don't. I drown it out with Elaine Paige and the menacing hum of me knitting machine.
VINNIE	I threw an egg at Margaret Thatcher once.

ROY Who?

VINNIE Roy please don't say things like that.

MATT Did you hit her?

VINNIE Hit her? I nearly killed her. It was a Cadbury's Crème Egg.

ROY It's not my fault I speak like I do. Blame me Mam and Dad for bringing us up in Barnoldswick.

BO Found a posy yet Carm?

CARMEL I'm having trouble getting out of this site on vinegar.

BO Oh. www.vinegarsgreat.com? I love that site!

Matt notices Roy is sitting, lost in thought, frowning.

MATT What's the matter Roy? Is the telly freaking you out?

ROY No I were just thinking. I was on the bus before, right. And we slowed down. And I seen this sign in the street. Slow Children Crossing. And I looked at the kids. And they didn't look a bit slow. Int life cruel? It's labels like that that stick with you forever.

MATT Did people call you slow when you were a kid?

ROY All the time.

BO Think I might pop a note through. Ask her if she could perhaps end her lifelong romance with smelly veg.

CARMEL Did you know you can clean a kettle with vinegar?

BO	Brings it up a treat. And windows.
ROY	They said me Mam were slow. They said me Dad were slow. And they said I were slow. I wrote a poem about it when I went to Their Claire's creative writing class. It was called,. We're Not Slow, We Just Take Our Time.
BO	Every time I breathe in I want to gag.

They all sit there for a while.

CARMEL	Tin-Tin said that about me this morning.
BO	Tin-Tin wants to count his blessings. So what if you've rampant halitosis Carm? You're pretty with it. Specially round the eyes.
CARMEL	He goes "Hey you fat cow, I hope you're gonna lose weight for the wedding. Or else you're on your own in them snaps'.
BO	Oh just do what every other bride in the country does. Take a dangerously high level of amphetamines. You watch. Your saddle bags'll drop off.
CARMEL	S'pose.

After a while.

ROY	Think I'll practice me driving again. Vinnie. Will you slap your hand on the dashboard at some point so I can practice me emergency stop?
VINNIE	What's your dashboard?
ROY	It's like this thing at the front of the car and...
VINNIE	This?!!

He indicates the arm of the sofa. Roy nods.

Vinnie returns to reading.

ROY   Mirror. Signal. Manoeuvre.

And Roy mimes driving again. After a while.

ROY   *(To Vinnnie)* Are you reading Harry Potter?

*Vinnie shows him the cover of his book,
showing he is not reading Harry Potter.
He then continues to read.*

ROY   Er, Vinnie? You haven't answered my
question!

VINNIE   *(Vinnie looks at him incredulous)* Yes Roy. I'm
reading Harry Potter and the Ring of Fire.

ROY   Is it true he's got a mate called Haemorhoid?

*Vinnie slaps the arm of the sofa aggressively.
Roy shrieks and 'does an emergency stop'.*

VINNIE   Yes Roy. Haemorhoid Blue.

ROY   God.

CARMEL   Famous vinegar drinkers include Jesus
Christ, son of God no less.

BO   Really? I always thought he was a wine buff.
Oh maybe it's that cider vinegar, eh.

ROY   I thought our Tracey were winding us up.

BO   Oh how is your Tracey Roy? Is she still
suffering terribly from depression?

ROY   Yeah. She just hangs round the house all day
watching Trisha and saying things like
'There's no point to life. All I can see are vistas
of desolation and nothingness'.

VINNIE   Apart from that she's great.

BO	D'you think it's post-natal?
ROY	No, I think it's coz she's recently had a baby. And it's quite an unfortunate looking child. I mean, in a way, I can sort of understand where she's coming from. But then, what d'you expect when the dad's pig ugly and she's no oil painting? Two wrongs don't make a right do they?
BO	They certainly don't make an attractive child.
ROY	Still, I've prettied her up as much as I can. Done her hair like Catherine Zeta Jones in Chicago.
BO	Bob?
ROY	No, Catherine Zeta Jones.
VINNIE	Roy. Could we try something new here?
ROY	Sushi? I've had it. Loads o'times.
VINNIE	Could we maybe try having five minutes when we don't speak?
ROY	I go on, don't I?
VINNIE	I just think it might help with your concentration on your driving. Okay?
ROY	Ah, you look out for me Vinnie don't you?
VINNIE	I'm all heart Roy.
	They sit there in silence for a few seconds. Roy 'drives'. After a while he mimes switching off a button.
ROY	*(To Vinnie)* Radio off.
	Bo has been writing a note for her neighbour. She reads it aloud now.

BO	Listen to this. Dear Feroza. Eleven words to say to you darl: Don't like the smell of cabbage. Hurry up and eat it. All best, Bojangles. P.S. You still don't appear to have returned the egg slicer I leant you on April the 18th.
CARMEL	I thought you said you'd seen it on Ebay?
BO	I could never prove it.

And then the doorbell rings. The lads all sit up and Bo inspects the CCTV. Carmel peers at the screen, then the others.

BO	This one's quite effeminate.
CARMEL	He's got a look of Sherrie Hewson.
VINNIE	It is Sherrie Hewson.
BO	Oh I've switched over to Loose Women by mistake.

She changes channels.

BO	Whoever it is they've bought lunch.
ROY	Oh it'll be my pizza bloke. Is it the redhead?
BO	Difficult to tell without my specs.
VINNIE	And the fact that it's a black and white telly.
BO	Actually he's got a look of Friar Tuck.
ROY	Oh no, the one I fancy looks like the bloke out o'Robin Hood.
VINNIE	Roy? Just go and answer the door.
CARMEL	Sure it's not my Tin-Tin?
ROY	How do I look?

MATT   Just go!

Roy exits. After a while.

VINNIE   Wanker.

MATT   I prefer the term prostitute.

Vinnie grimaces at Matt. Carmel is still looking at the screen.

CARMEL   It's not Tin-Tin is it?

BO   He doesn't look seething enough to be Tinny, now. I'm popping next door.

(Licks the envelope) I'm not even going to mention the Knowsley Safari Park novelty Back Scratch I chucked over the fence when she got those scabies.

And off she goes.

WHAT HAPPENS NEXT?
CAN YOU HAVE THE LAST LAUGH?

Some Day I'll Find Me

by Carla Lane

© Carla Lane

CARLA LANE

*Carla is the grand-dame of the sitcom world.
She broke into the almost exclusively male world
of sitcom writing with The Liver Birds in 1969.*

*Born in Liverpool, her home town and its culture
has always featured strongly in her writing.
Carla's major credits include Butterflies and
Bread which centred on the Boswell family.
Outside of her writing she is a staunch animal
rights activist and owns and runs a large animal
sanctuary in Sussex and a small island off the
coast of Wales where birds which have been
affected by oil spillages can be released into
a safe, wild environment.*

SCENE 1

Ext. a small detached house – it's own garden.

This is in a road with like houses. A car is parked in the drive. We hear loud pop music coming through the open bedroom window. The front door opens and Alwyn comes rushing out. Her coat is open, her face is fraught. She hastily gets into the car and drives out fast.

SCENE 2

Ext. on road further on.

The car is speeding – see Alwyn's tense face.

SCENE 3

Ext. country road.

The car is speeding – Alwyn's face.

SCENE 4

Ext. top of hill.

There is complete silence. Alwyn comes over the top of the hill towards us. She stops. She is quiet for a moment to get herself together. She spreads out her arms and utters a loud frustrating scream.

SCENE 5

Int. house, kitchen.

We hear loud music. Gwen is sitting by the table, she is eating a biscuit and gyrating to the music. She is dressed in a very modern way with most of her body showing.

Lill enters with her hoover. She plugs it in.

GWEN   *(Switches off radio)* Don't switch that on, my nerves are shattered.

     Lill takes a duster out of her pocket and begins to dust around.

GWEN   Don't do that – my lungs are organic.

LILL   *(Deadpan)* Will your throat panic if I have a fag?

GWEN   Just wait until I've gone, will you.

     Lill sits opposite her at the table. After a pause and a little feeling of uneasiness.

LILL   Listen Miss Gwen.

GWEN   *(Stops dancing)* My name is not Gwen. I am going to be a popstar – my name is Letice.

LILL   Look, I've been with your Mam for a long time.

GWEN   Not as long as I have.

LILL   I don't like to see her unhappy.

GWEN   *(Now absorbed in a modern magazine and not really listening)* Who in their right mind would take an innocent baby and call it Gwen?

     Lill goes to speak.

     Even that deranged cat next door, the one that climbs on the bird tray to get to the clothes line so it can pee on the washing, is called Esmeralda.

LILL   Anyway, what I wanted...

     She stops.

GWEN   But I have to go through my life called Gwen.

LILL   Why don't you use your full name –
        Gwendoline?

GWEN   *(Irritated)* Because I don't want people to
        think I'm related to Windolene.

        Lill goes to speak again.

GWEN   Look I don't want to hear any more. You can
        rap if you like, but I'm out of it – not listening
        – gone – OK.

LILL   *(Quietly)* She's very unhappy.

GWEN   She's had her youth – I'm trying to have mine.

LILL   She's trying to guide you, it's a mother's job.

GWEN   Look, I've got a voice. I'm going to use it. And
        I am going to be a popstar.

LILL   It's a fake world, the popstar world. They've
        all got plastic teeth, plastic gums and plastic
        breasts. Their lips look as if they've been to
        the garage air pump. They don't eat. I bet half
        of them have to put wire mesh over the bath
        plughole.

GWEN   I'm not listening.

LILL   By the time they're twenty, they'll be using a
        stairlift.

GWEN   Look, I paid dearly for my talent. Before I was
        born I lay there in that storm tossed uterus,
        listening to my Mam and Dad screeching at
        each other. It was like listening to Madam
        Butterfly and Old Man River. It's a good job
        my Mam won all the arguments. I could have
        come out a baritone.

She gets up and leaves, saying:

How sad is that.

LILL   *(Mutters)* Arrogant little cow.

SCENE 6

Int. Leo's flat – kitchen.

Silence as Alwyn and Leo sit opposite each other. There is a large home made trifle on the table. Yhe letter "b" has already been written in cream on top of it.

LEO   *(Eventually)* Look, I know we are incompatible, but isn't it time we came to a friendly oasis? A time of acceptance, a time of talking, a time of hope?

            Long pause.

ALWYN   I hate you.

LEO   Well, I suppose that's a start.

ALWYN   I don't like the tone of your voice. I don't like that "little boy hurt" look on your face when it suits you, and I don't like the general way Mother Nature has put you together.

LEO   I'm sorry, I know, I know, I'm just an ugly bastard.

ALWYN   And your right shoulder is higher than the left – that means you're in the mood for a fight.

LEO   It does not mean that I'm in the mood for a fight. It means I am deformed.
            (Pause). As well.

ALWYN   I know all the signs – I lived with them for
           years.

LEO   *(Sighs)* Instead of making little verbal darts
           and piercing each other with them, couldn't
           we...

ALWYN   *(Screeching)* You installed me in a little flat.

LEO   I did, yes. It's all I could afford. But now
           you're in a big house and I'm in a little flat.

ALWYN   You made me pregnant.

LEO   Yes, I did. You make it sound as if I crept up
           on you with a test tube.

ALWYN   I wanted a boy.

LEO   Oh, well, why didn't you say?

ALWYN   You persuaded me to give up a good job.

LEO   I wanted to look after you.

ALWYN   No, you wanted me to stay at home so I could
           look after you.

           He goes to speak.

ALWYN   And, not satisfied with that, you anchored me
           down with a daughter, not an ordinary "hello
           Mummy, hello Daddy, I love you to bits"
           daughter, but a female Satan who goes around
           with ironmongery hanging from her ears, her
           nose, her belly button and I dread to think
           where else.

LEO   She's young – it's the fashion – she'll grow
           out of it.

ALWYN   She's complaining about her chest. She says she can get a better cleavage with her shoulder blades.

LEO   I'll talk to her.

ALWYN   All the values, all the subtlety, all the things my mother taught me – keep your knees together – don't show your knickers – and when a man offers you a sweet you say "thank you".

He gives a big sigh.

ALWYN   This world is all sex, all violence and carnivorous kissing.

He goes to speak again.

Anyway, I share some of her thoughts. I'm not all that pleased with my own breasts. You always said that they were less frightening than most.

LEO   You're 43.

ALWYN   Don't give me all that "you're too old" crap, Leo.

LEO   I like you the way you are.

ALWYN   But not as much as Barbara Williams.

LEO   Don't be silly. I work with her. So she sent me a birthday card.

ALWYN   Oh yes, I know. I remember the verse. "When the sky is blue, when the sun comes through. When flowers unfold and the moon is gold. I think of you".

LEO   She's over emotional.

ALWYN   She's oversexed. I think I might join these mod, cool, "yea man" people. I've never liked my nose. I'll have fat sucked out of my thighs, my bottom hoisted up and...

LEO   You haven't mentioned your eyes.

ALWYN   What's wrong with my eyes?

LEO   Well, you were always complaining that they were too small. Perhaps they'll fix you up with one big one in the middle.

He laughs gently behind his hand. He is trying to be funny and to make friends.

ALWYN   It's nothing to laugh about, Leo. We both agreed.

LEO   I know, I know, that if our marriage became...

He is stuck for a word.

ALWYN   Unbearable is the word you're looking for.

LEO   Right, if our marriage became unbearable, we'd live apart and just stay good friends and see if we really needed a divorce.

She looks at him for a long time, and then:

ALWYN   You're still making trifles I see.

LEO   Yes, yes, I like making trifles.

ALWYN   It's a weird thing for a man to do.

LEO   Chef's do it a lot.

ALWYN   But you're not a chef, you're a boring accountant. Why couldn't you have been an airline pilot or a mountaineer?

LEO   I don't like heights, the way you don't like water.

Alwyn is looking at the trifle. Pause.

ALWYN   At least I tried.

LEO   Oh yes I remember, the Life Guard had to fly in and lift you out of the paddling pool.

ALWYN   You used to put my initials on your trifles.

LEO   Oh God, don't start again. Let's have some coffee?

He goes to make coffee and while he's doing this, she picks up the cream bag and finishes the word beginning with "b" by writing "bastard" across the trifle.

She walks out.

SCENE 7

Int. Alwyn's house, kitchen.

Music can be heard coming from upstairs.

Alwyn sits at the table, her coat still on, her head in her hands.

Lill puts a cup of tea in front of her.

ALWYN   Thanks Lill, thanks.

Lill goes across the kitchen, goes to a cupboard, takes out a packet of biscuits.

Alwyn is too immersed in her problems to look at her.

ALWYN   I'm sorry, I'm having a bad day.

(Pause) Again.

Lill is trying to tear the biscuit wrapping off but it won't give. She tries her teeth.

CU of Alwyn.

ALWYN   Isn't it weird, this life. This allotted time we have – I mean how can we possibly fit everything in without making a mess of most of it? You've got adolescence, middle-age, old age and finally you die.

We cut briefly to Lill who is still struggling with the packet of biscuits.

You lie in a box made from wood, pinched from the rain forest, surrounded by genetically engineered flowers. They wipe off all the disappointments and all the frustrations from your brow, and you go to your grave looking as if you are a Botox addict.

Cut to Lill. biscuits are all over the floor now. She runs round picking them all up, puts them on a plate, takes them across to Alwyn.

LILL   What did you say?

ALWYN   It's alright, it's alright.

Lill plonks the plate on the table.

LILL   No wonder there's a lot of violence about – it's all this plastic wrapping, you'd have to be a bloody terrorist to open them.

Alwyn closes her eyes and sighs. The music upstairs suddenly stops.

Gwen comes bursting into the room.

GWEN   As you know I'm going to be a pop star, I'm going to be famous, I'm going to be rich so let me show you my latest routine, it's cool, it's wicked.

Pause. It's wicked.

She switches on a small recorder.

LILL   I don't know how her chest takes all that banging about. It's a wonder she doesn't knock herself out.

Gwen continues her dance. It is very sexy and we have exaggerated close ups of various parts of her anatomy.

Lill raises her eyes to heaven and walks out muttering:

LILL   Oh God, bless us and save us.

Alwyn watches in horror, as she wriggles her bottom and shakes her chest, rolling her eyes, pouting her lips. It all suddenly stops.

GWEN   Do you like it?

ALWYN   I, er, I, think, it's, it's, no I don't.

Gwen sits opposite her at the table.

GWEN   Hey, come on – it's fantastic. It's cool.

ALWYN   It's not what I had in mind for you.

GWEN   Oh, I get it. You wanted me to meet a nice, kind guy and have a nice white wedding and lots of nice pink babies.

ALWYN   No, no. I'm a modern thinking woman – nothing shocks me. I think when I watch television, I think that's the way it is – people go naked and say bad words.

GWEN   Bad words – what bad words?

ALWYN   Well, I can't say them cos they're bad.

ALWYN   *(Quickly)* Nothing shocks me, nothing. Oh, except kissing. Kissing shocks me. Not doing it, but watching it. All that open mouth stuff, all that tongue groping – it's more like a culinary experience than a kiss.

GWEN   Yeah, well we're up front aren't we.

ALWYN   What happened to all that private sweet lip to lip stuff?

GWEN   There's no time for all that crap. Life's bus runs every two minutes now and you've got to run like hell and catch it.

ALWYN   Well I was thinking of changing things, now that your father has left. Sort of catching up. I thought I might put my life together in a sort of cool pattern, sort of trendy.

GWEN   You're 43!

ALWYN   So what's wrong with 43?

GWEN   Well it's that funny time isn't it, when your hormones are all rushing towards the exit.

                I suppose if you go on HRT you might make it.

ALWYN   I don't need HRT.

GWEN   It's great stuff. All my friends' mums are on it.
         It gives you that wow factor, that aggro.

ALWYN   I don't need aggro – I've got your father.

         Lill reappears.

LILL   Excuse me Miss Lettuce.

         Gwen immediately furious.

GWEN   Letice, not lettuce, I'm not a fucking salad.

LILL   Whatever.

         *Alwyn grabs Gwen by the shoulders. speaks
         close to her face.*

ALWYN   Don't you ever use that word in this house.

         They stare at each other.

GWEN   They use it on television.

         Alwyn tightens her grip.

ALWYN   They murder people on television.

         *After another stare she releases Gwen who
         runs out of the room. Alwyn is shocked by her
         own rage. Sudddenly she breaks out of it.*

ALWYN   *(To Lill)* Now she's suggesting I go on HRT.

LILL   I went on that once, but it made my head
         think about things my body couldn't cope
         with.

         (As she clears the table) Perhaps you should
         talk to her Dad a bit more.

ALWYN   No, not yet. When he can't get his head
         around something, he froths and stutters –
         you end up having to give him the kiss of life.

LILL   Aye, it's alright as long as somebody's
            listening.

ALWYN   What a terrible name, Letice.

LILL   Aye, well they all have funny names don't
            they. I mean, look at Meat Loaf, enough to
            make you go vegetarian.

ALWYN   You know, Lill, sometimes I blame myself.

            (Pause) Sometimes I think I want to hurt Leo.
            I don't mean physically, I don't mean punch
            him or anything like that.

LILL   Oh, I'd love to punch my fella. He's too pissed
            to stand still enough.

ALWYN   I imagine him coming back into the house and
            finding me writhing about on the sofa with
            another man.

LILL   Aye well, we all fantasise. When I clean
            around the house, I imagine I'm hoovering up
            my fella's ashes.

ALWYN   But you've had six children to him.

LILL   Yeah, but they've all left now. Well, except our
            Billy. The rest are just wandering around the
            universe, smoking, drinking and procreating.

ALWYN   I'm sure you were a super Mum.

LILL   I was. I did everything for them, everything.
            Our Billy went off to London, didn't leave a
            note, didn't phone. Our Jimmy, the eldest
            went down to talk to him – Paddington it was
            – London. His mate opened the door. "Can I
            see our Billy", he said. "He's gone", he said,
            "Moved on. He had that many plastic syringes

	sticking out of him, he looked like a chandelier".
ALWYN	Oh Lill, I'm so sorry.
LILL	It's alright, he's home now. He's given up that sort of useless life. He gets pissed with his Dad now.
ALWYN	I'm sorry Lill, I'm truly sorry. I didn't know how hard life has been for you. Leo was good you see. I just – we just – it's just that – he's...
LILL	A fella, I know – you can't have a better defence than that. (*She wanders out.*)
	Alwyn is thoughtful. she puts her head back in the chair and closes her eyes.

SCENE 8

Int. Alwyn's house.

Alwyn is still sitting in the chair but is listening to some really miserable classical music.

She hears the front door open.

Leo comes in. She looks at him and closes her eyes again.

LEO	(*Awkwardly*) The dying swan, good cheerful stuff.
	Nothing from Alwyn.
	(*Awkwardly*) I came to say, er, I'm sorry we've ended up like this, and to assure you that Barbara...
	She opens her eyes.

... is just a friend. We don't, we don't...

(Pause)... do anything.

ALWYN   You mean, you don't have sex.

LEO   That's right, that's it, yes.

ALWYN   Anymore?

LEO   Anymore, yes – no.

ALWYN   So, it's over?

LEO   Yes, no, it never began.

She closes her eyes and rocks to and fro.

LEO   I'm growing tired of this situation now.

ALWYN   I'm frightened Leo.

He is concerned. He sits down.

I'm frightened of how much time has passed. *(Pause)*. I looked at my feet the other day, they're so ugly.

LEO   I can tolerate your feet.

ALWYN   They rose out of the bath like some great sea monster. And my arms – they are flabby, like wings. I could launch myself off a rock and do a world tour with them.

Leo goes to speak.

ALWYN   *(Suddenly a great wail)* I miss my mother.

We see a short clip of Leo and Alwyn being served dinner by Alwyn's mother. When she gets to Leo's plate she serves his portion of mashed potato from a great height. It lands in the gravy and splashes his shirt.

Back to Alwyn, tearful.

LEO   A lovely lady your mother.

ALWYN   And my dog – I miss my dog.

We see a scene of Leo pressed with his back to his car, the dog is growling at him.

Leo is quite terrified.

LEO   He was a lovely, gentle dog, yes.

ALWYN   He'd have been a lot lovelier if you hadn't reversed over him.

LEO   I did not reverse over him. He crawled beneath my car thinking he had access to my feet.

ALWYN   He never got over it.

LEO   *(Losing his cool)* Nor did I. You screamed so loudly, you frightened him and he got my arse.

ALWYN   It's no use, I can't have a conversation with you. You've changed. You used to have a nice smile. I always looked forward to your smile, now it's all begrudged, a chimp has a better smile than you.

LEO   Maybe he's having a better life than me.

ALWYN   Go on, blame me for your terrible life.

LEO   *(Leo sighs)* This can't go on, can it.

ALWYN   No, it can't.

LEO   What should we do?

Alwyn just shrugs her shoulders.

SCENE 9

Int. psychiatrist's consulting room.

Alwyn is lying on a psychiatrist's couch.

The lady psychiatrist draws up another chair.

ALWYN   *(Nearly tearfully)* I came because I'm muddled.

PSYCH   *(Low soothing voice)* Right, now I want you to relax. I want you to talk to me. Talk as if I was your friend. Be free with it. I want to hear all of your thoughts and fears, things which made you happy, things which made you sad, even things which made you frightened. So close your eyes and just talk.

SCENE 10

Int. Alwyn's house – living room.

Lill is going round slapping everything with her duster. She is singing in a rather high pitched voice – an aria.

Gwen comes bursting into the room.

GWEN   Do you mind, I'm trying to practise upstairs. Who do you think you are – Maria Callas?

LILL   *(Deadpan)* She's dead.

GWEN   I know she's dead – just let her rest in peace will you.

As Gwen rushes back up the stairs.

LILL   She was a real singer, not like you lot – she didn't need skirts up to her navel and a Grand Canyon cleavage.

The door slams upstairs.

LILL   She had a voice.

The phone rings. Lill goes towards it muttering.

Alright, alright. I've got arthritic knees and my thermals are riding up.

(Picks up phone) Hello.

MALE VOICE   Hi sexy.

Gwen's voice (on upstairs phone, sexy too)

Hi.

Lill puts the phone down and mimics her.

LILL   Hi. *(She mutters)* Well, she might as well enjoy herself before she needs a hip replacement.

She wanders about flapping the duster again. the front door is opened and Leo lets himself in.

LEO   Hello Lill, is Alwyn about?

LILL   No.

LEO   Any clues?

LILL   No.

LEO   How is she then?

LILL   Apart from terminal depression, she's fine.

LEO   Depressed, why is she depressed?

LILL   I think it's got something to do with being alive.

LEO   You're not going to be very helpful are you?

LILL   No.

LEO	You don't like me do you?
LILL	No.
LEO	Could we talk about that?
LILL	No.
LEO	I see. It's girls together is it.
	No reply.
	I'll er, I'll go then.
	No reply.
LEO	Tell her I called will you?
	No reply.
	He leaves hesitantly.
LILL	*(To herself)* Tosser.

SCENE 11

Int. psychiatrist's consulting room.

CU of Alwyn's face. It is strained. Over the shot, psychiatrist tearful and heartbroken.

PSYCH   *(Dramatically)* So, here we are – separate and yet not separated. Married but only on paper. Neither of us knows what's wrong and neither of us knows how to put it right.

I tried so hard. I even went to his stupid Masonic evenings wearing a stupid pink frock, stupid pink lipstick and a bloody stupid pink flower thrust between my breasts.

(More crying) I did love him once, and now I am missing all the things I hated. The way he'd sit watching TV with his bare feet propped up in the fruit bowl. They way he ate chips, sort of slowly sucking them in. He did it so deliberately that I actually felt sorry for the chips. *(Pause)* But he had a gentleness – an awkwardness.

She can't speak now, she is sobbing too much.

PSYCH   *(Cont.)* He, he...

CU of Alwyn's face, eyes to heaven.

ALWYN   *(Quietly to herself)* Oh shit.

SCENE 12

Int. Alwyn's house.

The phone is ringing in the hall. Lill picks it up.

LIL   Hello.

MAN'S VOICE   Oh, hi. Latice?

LILL   She's in bed.

MAN   Any idea when she's likely to surface?

LILL   No.

MAN   OK. Would you tell her that Laurient called?

LILL   Who?

MAN   Laurient. Her Agent. I'll ring later. OK cool.

LILL   *(Dryly)* Cool man.

She puts phone down. Plods to the kitchen.

Alwyn is sitting drinking coffee and is turning the pages of a woman's magazine.

ALWYN   Who was it?

LILL   Someone for Lettuce.

ALWYN   Latice.

LILL   Aye, whatever.

The phone rings again.

ALWYN   I'll get it.

LILL   *(Mutters as she potters around the kitchen)* That bloody phone.

Alwyn picks up the phone.

ALWYN   Hello.

NANCY   Hi. A voice from the past.

(Pause) Hailsham, Nancy Hailsham.

ALWYN   *(Sudden realisation)* Nancy, I can't believe it. All these years.

NANCY   Yeah. Well I hear on the grapevine that you're on the loose.

ALWYN   Well, not on the loose exactly. Leo and I are living separately for a while, trying to sort things out.

NANCY   That's great, that's cool. It still qualifies you. You remember Jenny, Hazel, Sheila.

ALWYN   And Queenie.

NANCY   Yeah, and Queenie. Well, we're all divorced.
          That is except Hazel, she's a widow. But
          anyway, we're all manless and we meet up
          once a week at the Lantern Restaurant.
          Do you know it – in Keel Street?

ALWYN   By that old pub?

NANCY   Yeah, I know it. Every Saturday, eight o'clock
          and we thought that being as you qualify now,
          you might like to join us.

ALWYN   Well, I'd love to see you all again. Poor Hazel,
          a widow.

NANCY   She's OK. Saved her getting a divorce.
          Anyway, we'll see you – Saturday, eight
          o'clock. Looking forward to it, honey. Bye then.

WHAT HAPPENS NEXT?
CAN YOU HAVE THE LAST LAUGH?

SOME DAY I'LL FIND ME BY CARLA LANE

Last Quango in Harris

by Laurence Marks & Maurice Gran

© Mike Prince

LAURENCE MARKS & MAURICE GRAN

Laurence and Maurice met in the Finsbury Park Company of the Jewish Lads' Brigade in 1960 and both are still awaiting their first promotion.

They became full-time scriptwriters in 1980, since when they have written a plethora of hit series, including: Birds of a Feather, Goodnight Sweetheart, Shine On Harvey Moon, Love Hurts, and The New Statesman. They have also written two flops, but are not prepared to name them.

They have recently written their first stage play, Playing God, which will premiere in 2005.

Their ambition is to travel and work with animals.

SCENE 1

Ext. Little Minch. Day one – morning.

A ferry boat chugs across this absurdly named stretch of sea between Scotland and the Isle of Harris. Robin Crews, our hero, stands by the rail, gazing towards his new island home. He is 27, reasonably good looking, and so unsure what to do with his life that he became a civil servant.

Over this scene we hear the inimitable tones of Rod's Stewart's classic hit "Sailing". After a few choruses, the captain – a wiry, mustachioed, vicious-looking individual in naval uniform – storms out of the wheel house, snatches a large portable radio/cd player from the passenger it belongs to, and hurls the offending radio into the sea. Rod gurgles into silence.

SCENE 2

Ext. T.R.L.C. offices. Day one – afternoon.

An official looking sign tells us this is the "Tartan Registration and Licencing Commission". It is housed in a collection of 1950s prefabricated buildings on the edge of the remotest village on the Island of Harris.

A brand new Mercedes pulls up, with a big sticker on the door that reads "Death Taxis, Isle of Harris". On closer inspection it's "De'ath Taxis", for the driver is a Mr De'ath, a wiry, mustachioed, vicious-looking individual in jeans and a leather jacket. Oddly enough, he is a dead ringer for the ferry's captain.

Robin gets out of the back seat. The boot opens remotely, he removes his copious luggage. De'ath stays put, with no intention of helping.

SCENE 3

Int. T.R.L.C. offices. day one – moments later.

The office is open-plan, but the furniture is old, wooden and solid, and the computers are hefty and virtually obsolete. At one end of the office there's a table with electric kettle, mugs, tea making requisites etc. In the middle of the room is a big heavy commercial photocopying machine. At the far end is a small glassed-in office, belonging to Geoffrey Amhurst, the Head of the Commission.

We open as Geoffrey – an avuncular chap of 58 – is giving Robin the guided tour, weaving between desks where the other staff – two women, one man, all clearly bored and unmotivated – barely pretend to work.

GEOFFREY   ... that's Alice, and last but not least, Angela.

         The two women look at him with hostile curiosity.

GEOFFREY   *(Cont'd)* Of course, this place used to be something of a backwater...

         We find we can hear what Robin is thinking.

ROBIN   *(In his head)* Used to be?

GEOFFREY   But suddenly, between Burberry and Jean Paul Gaultier, tartan is the new black. Fresh designs started springing up everywhere. Obviously the powers that be couldn't let that sort of thing go unregulated.

ROBIN   *(Aloud)* Of course not.

         (In his head) When's the next boat out of here?

GEOFFREY   So have you always been keen on tartan?

ROBIN	Well... I saw Braveheart twice.
GEOFFREY	*(Scornfully)* Braveheart! What an anachronistic farrago; Mel Gibson sporting a McTavish tam o'shanter three hundred years too early!
ROBIN	That's Hollywood for you.
GEOFFREY	Quite. Now this will be your desk...

Geoffrey shows Robin to the furthest desk.

ROBIN	What exactly am I supposed to do?
GEOFFREY	No hurry, you just get yourself settled in. Julian will show you the ropes presently, won't you Julian?

Julian Uxbridge, a shock haired, neurotic 30 year old at the next desk looks up.

JULIAN	If I had a rope don't you think I'd have hanged myself by now?
GEOFFREY	That's the spirit!

(To Robin) You've got to laugh, haven't you? Now, one more thing; Your staff report said you're a non-smoker?

ROBIN	Yes, why?
GEOFFREY	Only we all smoke here.
ROBIN	It's a free world.
JULIAN	*(Sarcastically)* Huh!
GEOFFREY	So when we light up, if you wouldn't mind standing outside the door?

Geoffrey goes back to his room. A bemused Robin sits at his desk.

He has no idea what to do, so he goes through the drawers and finds some rubber stamps, faded stationery, a mouldy half-eaten apple, a football rattle and a ring-binder with "authorised tartans" printed on the front. He opens it. It's full of black and white photocopies of different tartans – in shades of grey, of course.

JULIAN   So what did you do to get sent here?

ROBIN   They said it was a promotion.

JULIAN   *(Bitterly)* That's what they said to me. I was so naive.

Then Robin notices that a woman of 60, Alice Sackville-East, is making tea. Robin crosses to her.

ROBIN   Any chance of a cup?

ALICE   You tell me.

ROBIN   Sorry?

ALICE   As you can see, there are four mugs, tallying almost uncannily with the number of persons employed here prior to your arrival. If you have a cup, mug or other heat-resistant receptacle about your person, I would be happy to fill it with tea, once you have made your contribution to the tea fund: viz £1.50, which includes two digestive or one fancy shortbread biscuit per break.

Julian and the third staffer, stringy, serious 40 year old Angela Underhill, gather for their tea. Both nod in support of Alice.

ROBIN   Couldn't I borrow one of your mugs, when
              you've finished, obviously, sort of wash it up,
              and er...? Just this once?

              An appalled silence. Finally...

ANGELA   How long have you been a civil servant?

ROBIN   Four years.

ANGELA   Just a slow learner then.

ROBIN   Can I at least have a biscuit?

ALICE   Of course. We're not Nazis.

              *Robin reaches for the tartan tin of shortbread.
              Alice waves a finger.*

ALICE   *(Cont'd)* Uh-uh-uh... One pound fifty.

              *Robin digs out some change and pays. They
              watch him as he takes two plain biscuits and
              goes back to his desk. He gets out his mobile
              and starts to compose a text.*

JULIAN   That's a waste of time.

ROBIN   What?

JULIAN   No signal.

ROBIN   It says there is...

JULIAN   I know it says there is, but there isn't. Mobiles
              just don't work on Harris. Or the internet. Or
              the phones, quite often. Not sure about smoke
              signals. Might set myself alight and find out.
              Who were you trying to text?

ROBIN   Just my mum.

JULIAN   She can't help you now.

> *Robin smiles, the way you do to a nutter, and nibbles his dry biscuit. A crumb catches in his throat. He coughs. Rather pathetically.*

JULIAN   *(Kinder)* You can dunk in my tea if you like?

ROBIN   *(Hoarse)* Thanks.

> *Robin is about to dip his biscuit, but...*

JULIAN   Wait!

> *Julian produces a biscuit-shaped cage, made of paper clips.*

ROBIN   What's that?

JULIAN   A dunking cage. To prevent bits breaking off and falling into the tea. I invented it.

ROBIN   You're not exactly overworked, are you?

> *Offended, Julian drains his tea and puts the cage back in its drawer. Clearly dunking rights have been withdrawn.*
>
> *Then Geoffrey comes to his cubicle doorway, brandishing his telephone.*

GEOFFREY   Alice, can you come and talk some sense into this Russian chappy? He seems to think he can add a fluorescent lilac stripe to the McMoosie tartan without a T.R.34! Typical.

ROBIN   *(In his head)* Help.

SCENE 4

Int. Stormy Petrel Inn. Day one – day.

An old fashioned pub, with battle axes, claymores, deer heads, shields and swords on the walls.

Robin struggles in with his suitcases and packages. There are a few fishermen drinking at the bar, and an elderly weaver spinning tweed at his wheel in the corner. None of them seem very friendly.

Behind the bar is Freya Ingolfdottir. She's 30, gorgeous, white-blonde hair, superb figure, lovely smile. She runs the pub, which trebles as post office and local shop.

Right now, she is selling stamps and groceries to an old lady. Robin gets in line. She smiles at him.

FREYA   *(Slight and charming accent)* Hello, you must be Mr Crews.

ROBIN   *(Overwhelmed by her beauty)* How..?

FREYA   Vernon marked my card.

ROBIN   Who..?

FREYA   Vernon De'ath? The taxi driver – amongst other things...

ROBIN   Oh.

FREYA   Do you only speak in one-syllable words containing the letter "o"?

ROBIN   No!

            (In his head) You're just the most beautiful woman I've ever seen, and as a result I've regressed to the age of two.

FREYA   Your room's at the top of the stairs, on the
           right. Mine's on the left. Try not to get them
           mixed up. There's only the one bathroom, but
           don't worry, when I'm in there I always sing.
           Mostly Bjork songs.

ROBIN   Bjork?!

FREYA   She's from Iceland.

ROBIN   *(Robin's dam bursts)* I know who Bjork is!
           I've got every CD she ever made. I love her!
           I loved her when she was in the Sugar Cubes,
           I loved her when she went solo, I even loved
           her in that weird movie, and I thought she
           was amazing when she did that thing at the
           Olympics. In fact, I love everything to do
           with Iceland. Iceland is my passion.

FREYA   I'm from Iceland.

ROBIN   No? Wow!

           (In his head) Be still my beating trousers.

FREYA   From EyjafjarSarsysla.

ROBIN   I love EyjafjarSarsysla!

FREYA   You know EyjafjarSarsysla?!

ROBIN   I lived in EyjafjarSarsysla!

FREYA   No! Why?

ROBIN   I was at the university, researching the life
           and poetry of Jonas Hallgrimsson.

FREYA   I'm descended from Jonas Hallgrimsson!
           What's your favourite poem?

ROBIN   The Farmer In Winter.

FREYA   Mine too!

ROBIN   "Goddess of Drizzle, driving your big cartloads of mist across my fields...

FREYA   "Send me some sun and I'll sacrifice my cow...

ROBIN   "My wife...

FREYA & ROBIN TOGETHER   "My Christianity!"

They laugh in mutual delight. Then they realise De'ath has come in. He's dressed as a postman, and is waiting impatiently by the bar.

DE'ATH   Who do you have to fuck to get a drink round here?

FREYA   Me. But I'm busy.

So De'ath goes behind the bar and pours himself a large malt whisky. He glares at Robin.

ROBIN   I'll take... bags... up... *(Robin tails off and takes his luggage upstairs)*

DE'ATH   What was all that about?

FREYA   We were talking about Jonas Hallgrimsson.

DE'ATH   Another of your Reykjavik fancy Dans?!

FREYA   Jonas Hallgrimsson was one of Iceland's greatest poets!

(Teasing) They say Rabbie Burns stole many of Hallgrimmson's ideas...

DE'ATH   If they say it on this island they're haggis!

          He holds out his glass. She refills it. He knocks it back. Again. Then he picks up sack of post from behind the counter.

          (Cont'd) Right, no rest for the wicked.

          De'ath exits.

FREYA   And you'd know.

          Freya washes up some glasses. Julian comes in.

FREYA   *(Cont'd)* Good evening Julian.

JULIAN   What's good about it? What's evening about it?! It doesn't even get dark 'til 3am!

FREYA   The usual?

JULIAN   You call it the usual. I call it the cripplingly predictable.

          Freya puts on the counter a loaf of bread, a toilet roll, six eggs, a chicken, two tins of baked beans, a video of Kill Bill 2, a grapefruit, and a pint of lager with a whisky chaser.

FREYA   I've met the new guy. Seems okay.

JULIAN   Okay? Hasn't even got his own mug.

FREYA   He knows a lot about Iceland.

JULIAN   Does he? I find that intensely suspicious. I wouldn't be surprised if he's some sort of spy, sent to undermine our already fragile morale...

          At this point Robin returns from upstairs.

JULIAN   *(Cont'd)* All right Rob?

Robin is surprised that Julian is so friendly.

JULIAN   *(Cont'd)* Drink?

ROBIN   *(Sarky)* Am I allowed? I mean, I don't have my own tankard.

JULIAN   Freya, get this man a tankard.

FREYA   Coming right up.

Freya gets a brand new tankard out its box.

FREYA   *(Cont'd)* Do you prefer italic, Times Roman, or Helvetica sans serif?

ROBIN   What?

FREYA   For your monogram.

ROBIN   What do you recommend?

FREYA   Jonas Hallgrimsson always swore by Helvetica.

ROBIN   Helvetica it is then.

Freya gets a small electric engraving machine from under the bar, and expertly puts "RC" on the tankard.

FREYA   There. Now, let's baptise it. What's your tipple?

ROBIN   Vodka and tonic.

Freya doesn't bat an eyelid. She puts the tankard under the optic for a shot of vodka. Then uncaps a bottle of tonic.

Julian leads Robin over to a table.

JULIAN   Happy days, he said sarcastically.

          (Swigs beer) So, what did you really do to get sent to Harris?

ROBIN   I didn't do anything.

JULIAN   You must have done something. You can tell me.

ROBIN   *(Patiently)* I was at V.A.T. Glasgow; Grade 12. I got my Grade 11, and they sent me here. I didn't really want to come, but I didn't want to wait years for the next promotion round, so I thought, give it a go...

JULIAN   *(Suddenly combative)* You'll have to do better than that!

ROBIN   *(Taken aback)* What do you mean?

JULIAN   You know what I mean.

ROBIN   I have no idea what you mean.

JULIAN   Who really sent you?

ROBIN   I don't know his name, someone in Human Resources...

JULIAN   Have it your own way. But don't think you're going to get anything out of me! You can play your evil little mind-games on your own, matey!

          Julian knocks back his beer and chaser, and storms out, leaving his shopping on the table.

ROBIN   *(In his head)* What did I do...

          Freya comes over.

ROBIN   *(Cont'd)*

             (Still in his head, without a pause) Fantastic
             tits!

FREYA   Where's Julian?

ROBIN   *(Shrugs)* He went.

FREYA   Oh my God, his shopping! This can only mean
             one thing!

ROBIN   No supper for Julian?

             Freya runs out of the pub.

FREYA   *(O.S.)* Julian! Julian?!

             Robin decides he'd better go after her.

SCENE 5

Ext. Stormy Petrel Inn/harbour. Day one – continuous.

*The pub is near the jetty, where Julian is climbing out
of his clothes. Under them he wears a wetsuit. He pulls
from the passenger seat of his parked car an already
inflated blow-up horse with a hole in the middle for his
waist. He pulls the horse over his head.*

Freya comes running from the pub, Robin in her wake.

FREYA   Julian, don't be a fool...!

             *But Julian jumps into the sea and strikes out
             for the distant mainland, as Freya and Robin
             reach the jetty.*

ROBIN   *(Breathless)* Why?

             *A speedboat roars into view. a police
             speedboat, piloted by De'ath, in police uniform
             and life jacket.*

ROBIN   *(Cont'd)* Isn't that..?

FREYA   He's also police Sergeant De'ath.

     De'ath has a loud-hailer.

DE'ATH   Mr Uxbridge, return to shore immediately.

     Julian keeps swimming.

DE'ATH   *(Cont'd)* I repeat, for your own safety, return to shore. This is your final warning!

     De'ath produces a rifle.

ROBIN   Jesus!

     Julian keeps swimming. De'ath takes careful aim, and blows the head off the horse.

     Julian now has a pathetic shred of plastic round him. he starts to flail. He's not much of a swimmer.

DE'ATH   Next time I won't be aiming at the horse's head!

     De'ath laughs and powers away, drenching Julian with his spume. Julian goes under.

     Robin rips off his suit, shirt and shoes, and jumps into the sea. He swims powerfully towards Julian.

ROBIN   Hold on Julian! *(in his head)* She's going to think I am so-o sexy!

     Robin grabs Julian and starts to bring him in.

SCENE 6

Int. T.R.L.C. offices. Day one – moments later.

The office seems to be empty, but we can hear strange noises. Then we realise there is a huge hole in the ground, where the photocopier was. We look into the hole, and see Alice and Angela digging. The desks are against the door.

There's a knock on the door. they stop digging. Another knock. It's not in code. Alice hauls herself out of the hole. She's very dusty. She goes to the window and looks out.

ALICE   *(Fierce whisper)* It's Julian!

        Angela gets out of the hole. She is dirty too. They pull the lino over the hole, and the desks away from the door. Then she opens the door.

        In staggers Julian, still in wet suit, supported by Robin, in wet underwear and Freya's too-small bathrobe. Alice sums up the situation.

ALICE   *(Cont'd)* Julian! You running lickspittle of capitalism!

ROBIN   *(In his head)* What?!!

        Robin settles Julian into a chair, while Alice and Angela push the photocopier back over the hole.

        Alice gets out her silver cigarette case. She offers fags to Angela and Julian, and lights them for them. Then she lights up too.

ROBIN   *(Cont'd)* I'll just hang around outside shall I? Until you've finished smoking?

ALICE   Stay where you are!

        (To Julian) What happened?

ROBIN   He...

ALICE   I'll tell you what happened. You tried to swim to the mainland, didn't you?

JULIAN   I only...

ALICE   And De'ath intercepted you?

ROBIN   He could have killed...

ALICE   Now he'll start springing surprise searches on us!

     (To Julian) If he finds the tunnel, I'll have your bollocks!

ROBIN   Tunnel? We're miles from the mainland!

ANGELA   We always knew it's going to be a long haul.

ROBIN   Hold on! Is this one of those reality TV shows? Where everyone's an actor except me?

ANGELA   Don't be absurd.

ROBIN   Then what the hell is going on?!

     No reply.

ROBIN   *(Cont'd)* You owe me an explanation, I saved his life!

JULIAN   *(Sulky)* Don't expect me to thank you.

     A long beat

ALICE   All right. Look, what would you do with civil servants who embarrass or undermine the government, but who can't possibly be dismissed?

ROBIN   No-one's that unsackable. Ask Greg Dyke.

ALICE   I'm unsackable. I was the tea lady at 10 Downing Street for thirty seven years. Then the Soviet Union... *(sad)* collapsed, and they discovered I'd been a KGB mole the whole time. Ha! *(beat)* Obviously it was too mortifying for them to put me on trial, and they couldn't let me tell the world, so they sent me here to rot for the rest of my days.

ROBIN   You don't expect me to believe that, do you?

ANGELA   It's all true. She's a traitor. I, on the other hand, have always been a patriot, dedicated to the Defence of the Realm. But then, after twelve years in Weapons Research and Procurement, I discovered that our much vaunted Trident nuclear submarine programme was an utter fiction.

ROBIN   That's impossible! I've seen them on TV! Big black scary things!

ANGELA   Radio controlled scale models.

ROBIN   What?!

ANGELA   The multi-billion Trident budget was in point of fact spent on a network of luxurious nuclear shelters for government ministers and their fat-cat donors.

Robin shakes his head at the enormity of it.

ROBIN   What about you Julian? What did you do?

JULIAN   Don't ask.

ROBIN   I am asking.

ANGELA   He got someone pregnant. Someone very high up.

ROBIN   Who?

A beat.

Julian beckons Robin over and whispers a name to him. Robin's jaw drops.

ROBIN   *(Cont'd)* Tony must have been livid..!

JULIAN   And they didn't even consult me about the MMR jabs!

A beat while Robin lets it all sink in.

ROBIN   If all this really is true, why don't you go public?

ANGELA   You think we haven't tried?

ALICE   Our phones are tapped, the fax machine only receives, you can't send texts, the internet always seems to be down

(Wryly) for some reason...

ROBIN   This is like something out of Kafka.

JULIAN   Now you're getting it.

ROBIN   How about Geoffrey? What did he do wrong?

ALICE   We don't think Geoffrey's done anything. He's just what he seems, a kindly, unimaginative, middle-ranking civil servant who runs the T.R.L.C.

ROBIN   You aren't trying to tell me this tartan licensing nonsense is for real?

ALICE   Who knows? Geoffrey certainly thinks it is.

JULIAN   Unless he's a brilliant actor with a keen sadistic streak, and he's just toying with us?

	(Beat) Like you are.
ANGELA	What do you mean?
JULIAN	He's still playing the innocent.
ALICE	You're amongst friends now, Robin. You can tell us why you're here.
ROBIN	I didn't do anything!
	It's all too much for Robin. He starts to shake.
ANGELA	Are you all right? You're shivering.
ALICE	Delayed shock.
ANGELA	Hot sweet tea, that's the thing.
ALICE	You're right!
	Alice puts the kettle on. then...
ALICE	*(Cont'd)* Just a moment. Have you acquired a mug?
ROBIN	Not yet.
ALICE	In that case... sorry.
	She switches off the kettle.

SCENE 7

Int. Stormy Petrel Inn. Day one – moments later.

Robin enters, still looking crappy. The pub is empty except for the old weaver in the corner. Freya comes out from behind the bar, concerned.

FREYA	Sit here...
	She leads him over to a chair, and plugs in an electric fire.

Then she goes to the bar and pours a large rum into his tankard.

FREYA   *(Cont'd)* Drink.

Robin drinks. He starts to recover and warm up.

FREYA   *(Cont'd)* You were so brave. I love men who are brave.

ROBIN   *(In his head)* Result!

FREYA   In Iceland we equate courage with virility.

ROBIN   It was nothing.

      (In his head) Yesss!

FREYA   Robin, why are you here?

ROBIN   Alice wouldn't make me a cup of tea.

FREYA   I mean on Harris!

ROBIN   I keep telling everyone, I don't know! I've never done anything out of the ordinary...

FREYA   You can tell me; were you a courageous commando who witnessed atrocities and was about to blow the whistle?

ROBIN   No. I worked for Customs and Excise, V.A.T...

FREYA   Perhaps you challenged the tax return of a powerful yet shadowy organisation?

ROBIN   Afraid not. I once accidentally filled out an official form in lower case, but that's hardly a capital offence... You really think it's true? The Commission is a dumping ground for...?

FREYA   I don't think. I know. Vernon told me.

ROBIN Then why don't you tell the world, and help
those poor sods escape?

FREYA I daren't. I might be forced to leave the island.

ROBIN You want to stay here?

FREYA I love Harris. I love Harris in the spring time,
I love Harris in the fall... And I can never
return to EyjafjarSarsysla.

ROBIN Why not?

FREYA There's a price on my head.

ROBIN What did you do?

FREYA *(Shrug)* I committed a white collar crime.

ROBIN Like falsifying your VAT return?

FREYA More like killing a vicar.

ROBIN *(Very startled)* You what?

FREYA It was an accident. I didn't even know he was
a man of the cloth... well, we were both
naked...

ROBIN Huh!?

FREYA ... in a sauna. Everyone else had gone, and he
kept pestering me to flagellate him with the
birch twigs. You know how vicars are. In the
end I stormed out, slamming the door behind
me. I didn't know, but I slammed it so hard
the lock jammed. He was found next morning,
casseroled to death.

ROBIN No?!

FREYA   I jumped on the first boat out of Iceland,
               and ended up here. Of course the police
               are looking for me, but unless Vernon gives
               me away...

ROBIN   And he won't?

FREYA   He and I have an understanding.

ROBIN   Which is...?

FREYA   He understands I want to lie low on Harris,
               and I understand he wants to lie low on me.

ROBIN   Oh.

               (In his head) Bastard!

SCENE 8

Int. T.R.L.C. offices. Day two – morning.

*Robin comes in. The others are already there. He goes over
to the tea table, and takes a huge mug out of his briefcase.
It's twice the size of all the others. He puts it on the table,
then he troops morosely to his desk, and slumps into his
seat.*

JULIAN   I hate you.

ROBIN   Why?

JULIAN   You saved my life.

ROBIN   Don't mention it.

               Geoffrey comes over with a huge ring binder.

GEOFFREY   Morning. Sleep well?

ROBIN   No. I'm bitten to pieces.

GEOFFREY   You're getting on well with Miss Ingolfdottir then?

ROBIN   I mean the midges! They're everywhere! And it never gets dark, and my bed is narrow and lumpy, and there were all sorts of squelchy noises coming from the other bedroom...

GEOFFREY   Ah. That would be Freya and...

ROBIN   I'm quite aware of what it would be, thank you!

GEOFFREY   *(Wistful)* She used to be Miss Iceland, did you know? Still, plenty more fish in the sea,

           (Innocently) eh Julian?

JULIAN   Piss off.

GEOFFREY   *(Ignores Julian)* Now as I'm sure you know, there are over five thousand five hundred and three unique tartans, which makes it fairly difficult to devise new ones.

ROBIN   Fascinating.

           (In his head) Who gives a toss?

GEOFFREY   However, we've just received a very exciting application, personally supported by our own Prime Minister, from the most powerful family in the world...

ROBIN   The Murdochs?

GEOFFREY   No, the Presidents Bush – both of them! They're coming to the Highland Games to toss their cabers, and they want to be clad in their very own tartan. So – any ideas?

ROBIN   How about something thick and random, with a yellow streak?

GEOFFREY   Mmm, interesting, but not very traditional. No, I suggest you work your way through these and see if you get any inspiration.

Geoffrey turns to go.

ROBIN   I don't want to.

GEOFFREY   Beg pardon?

ROBIN   I don't want to devise tartans. I don't want to even look at tartans, I want to go home.

GEOFFREY   Ah. Feeling poorly?

ROBIN   I mean back to Glasgow. I shouldn't be here, it's all a bizarre cock-up. And I've checked Staff Code, I know I'm entitled to reject a promotion move and return to my previous grade and posting...

GEOFFREY   *(Put out)* Oh, I see. Well, I must say, I am disappointed. It's not as if you've given us much of a chance.

Robin shrugs.

GEOFFREY   *(Cont'd)* I'd rather hoped to groom you to eventually fill my shoes, because this bunch, well...

ROBIN   *(Determined)* I believe there's a ferry this afternoon.

GEOFFREY   Very well, clearly no point trying to change your mind. But I hope you aren't expecting a leaving present?

Geoffrey goes back to his office.

JULIAN   You really think you're going to get off this
          island that easily? "I believe there's a ferry
          this very afternoon..."

ROBIN   We'll see.

JULIAN   Yes we will. Because this place is like Hotel
          California. You can check out any time you
          like, but you can never leave.

SCENE 9

Ext. Stormy Petrel Inn/harbour. Day two – afternoon.

*A few locals and tourists are lining up to get on the ferry.
Robin is at the back of the wee queue, with his luggage.*

*Then De'ath strolls up. He's wearing a harbour master
outfit – blazer with gold buttons, white trousers, white
shoes, white captain's cap.*

He exchanges pleasantries with the queue.

Then he comes up to Robin.

DE'ATH   Going somewhere?

ROBIN   Yes. Home.

DE'ATH   I don't think so, Mr Crews by name but not
          by nature.

ROBIN   Look, it's a free world!

DE'ATH   Where did you get that notion?

          (Beat) Do you even have a ticket?

ROBIN   I'll get one on board.

          *De'ath puts his face very close to Robin's.
          Robin winces.*

DE'ATH   No way, sunshine. Tickets can't be purchased on board. They must be purchased in advance, from the Harbour Master.

ROBIN   *(Losing hope)* Who happens to be...?

DE'ATH   Do you think I dress like a poof for my health?

ROBIN   *(Humbling himself)* Mr Harbour Master, might I possibly purchase a one way ticket out of here?

DE'ATH   What do you think? (*De'ath smirks and strolls on*)

SCENE 10

Int. Stormy Petrel Inn. Day two – a little later.

A very fed up Robin enters. Freya is behind the bar, weighing potatoes for a housewife.

FREYA   *(To customer)* Just help yourself.

   She crosses to Robin.

FREYA   *(Cont'd)* How could you?!

ROBIN   What?

FREYA   Go! Without even saying anything?

ROBIN   I was going to phone when I got to the mainland...

FREYA   Only Vernon wouldn't sell you a ferry ticket? Did you really think it would be so easy to escape?

ROBIN   I only know I have to get away and find out why I was sent here!

FREYA   I thought you hadn't done anything?

ROBIN   I thought I hadn't done anything. But now,
         I just don't know any more... *(Tails off)*

         Freya grabs his arm.

FREYA   But don't you realise how long I have waited
         for someone who cares as much as I for the
         verses of Jonas Hallgrimsson? Even in
         EyjafjarSarsysla they prefer Pam Ayres
         nowadays!

ROBIN   What about De'ath?

FREYA   A brave warrior like you should be able to
         vanquish him, like Asgaut the Thrall in the
         Laxdaela Saga!

ROBIN   Asgaut wasn't acting alone! He was kinsman
         of Egil the axe wielder! Give me a break here!
         And I'm not a warrior, I'm a tax collector, and
         I've got to get off this island or I'll go as mad
         as the rest of you...

         (Beat) I didn't mean you...

FREYA   *(Hurt)* I know what I heard.

         (Beat) All right. Take my car, there's an
         unmarked track behind the pub that joins up
         with the back road to Stornaway...

ROBIN   Oh, bless you Freya. I'll never forget you.

         Robin goes. Freya looks downcast.

WHAT HAPPENS NEXT?
CAN YOU HAVE THE LAST LAUGH?

Annie's People

by Ian Pattison

© Chris Hulme

IAN PATTISON

Biography? How could I claim to know anyone well enough to write their biography, including me? I'm just an appetite in shoes, like everyone else. What I may safely state, with fear of contradiction, is that I am unhappy-go-lucky and Scottish. Which is to say, British. Britishness being, of course, a sort of folded collective pacamac we produce from our pockets in time of national celebration, or crisis, then fold away again and forget about until the next national celebration, or crisis.

In short, I am I. You are you. We are the Walrus. Goo goog a joo.

SCENE 1

Est. shot. Ext: day. BBC Television Centre.

SCENE 2

Int. day. (day 1) Television centre: Third floor.

Milo, a man of thirty five, is walking along a corridor. He wears a coat, has a black media type bag over his shoulder. His hair is dyed to hide premature grey. As he walks, we hear his voice over.

MILO (V.O.)   The cliché about clichés is that they become clichés because they're true. But that's just a cliché. Take the one comedians always use about why they became comics. They always say it began at school when they'd make bigger kids laugh to avoid being bullied. But I made bigger kids laugh at school. All that happened to me was that I got myself kicked to a pulp for being a creepy little smart ass. Maybe you knew a kid like that. Maybe you wonder what became of him. Maybe, just maybe, he ended up like me.

Milo stops outside an office door.

Laminate sign on door reads 'Writers Room.'

A handwritten sign below reads 'Leave your ego at the door.'

Milo takes a deep breath, opens the door, enters.

SCENE 3

Int. day. (Day 1). Writers room.

A medium sized open plan office.

There's a conference type table and chairs centre of the room. Two glass fronted offices are contained within the writer's room. The larger of these belongs to Cy Kallow, the producer. The other is Milo's, as head writer. We're in Milo's office. It's a semi-private space with no door, just a doorway. Milo is at his desk. There's a tape cassette machine before him. Milo takes a deep breath. He presses the start button on the tape machine. We hear a taped street interview situation in progress. A market research type interviewer is asking members of the public questions.

INT'VIEWER	Excuse me, do you watch a television show called 'Annie's People?'
MOTP 1	Annie's People? What about it?
INT'VIEWER	Do you like it?
MOTP 1	Not much. I haven't really watched it.
MILO	*(Exasperated)* I haven't watched it but I don't like it. Nice judging, Solomon.
INT'VIEWER	How about you, do you like Annie's People?
MOTP 2	Is that the show with the dog?
MILO	Here we go.
INT'VIEWER	It's a comedy drama about a woman called Annie. And her, uh, her people.
MOTP 2	Yeh, I know, but they did one with a dog.
INT'VIEWER	How about your friend?
MOTP 3	Yes, I saw that. The dog was cool.

Milo, sighs.

MILO   *(Exasperated)* Sixteen episodes and two Christmas specials! All they talk about's a mutt.

INT'VIEWER   But what about the show overall? Annie's People?

MOTP 3   Oh, you know... It's alright.

Milo turns down the volume.

MILO (V.O.)   So there you have it. My name is Milo Debenham. I have a dormant ulcer and a high cholesterol count. My hands shake and I suffer occasional palpitations. But it's all worth it. I make a show that's alright.

Milo looks at his shaking hands. He turns up the volume again.

MOTP 3   Will you bring back the dog?

MILO   No!

Milo jabs off the tape. Cy, the producer, a man in his early forties, leans in.

CY   You heard the tape?

MILO   I heard the tape.

CY   I've been thinking. We should bring back the dog.

MILO   Cy –

CY   The last Focus Group report was adamant. Fifty one percent of those interviewed loved him. If we brought him back and cut off one of his legs, the sympathy vote could push us up another couple of points.

MILO	Cy –
CY	Or maybe hack off an ear. A one eared mongrel with no tail and blind. Who could resist him?
MILO	Cy, what's that on your neck?
CY	*(Fingers neck)* Oh, another Saturday night badge of Filth. At my age, I'm not proud. But then I think how drones like you spend your weekends and my guilt melts away like black snow.
	(Covers love bite with shirt collar) What time's the meeting?
MILO	*(Looks at his watch.)* Now. Why?
CY	I'll fetch my surprise!
	Cy goes. Milo frowns, puzzled.

SCENE 4

The writer's room. Minutes later.

We're C.U. on Milo.

MILO	Mirthmakers, let us walk the line! Annie is in bed. She's feeling neglected. Pete looks up from his laptop. Pete says – 'A writer is like God. He creates everything, yet his existence is constantly questioned. So what's the comeback, team? What knock-em-dead zinger does feisty Annie hit him with?

We pull out to show –

The writers around the table.

There's four of them, including Milo.

Laura is mid twenties. Nat also. Dobbsy is male, sixties, pretending forties. They all have scripts open before them. Laura's forehead is on the table, resting on her script.

Milo beams at Dobbsy and Nat, hopefully. Nothing. Laura, head still on table, raises her hand.

MILO   Nat, oblige us.

Nat lifts Laura's head by the collar.

MILO   Yes, Laura?

LAURA   Her existence?

MILO   That's not a joke, is it, Laura, that's gender politics. Could we keep them out of this discussion please?

LAURA   You dragged them in, claiming God's a he.

MILO   Okay, have it your way. His or her existence is constantly questioned. Now what knockout zinger Does Annie — Yes, Nat?

NAT   I don't like it.

MILO   Don't like what, Nat?

NAT   That line. 'The writer creates everything yet his existence is constantly questioned.' It sounds like a whine. It's anal.

MILO   An anal whine and we're only on page three. Might we raise the tone?

NAT   I just don't see why we writers should portray ourselves as victims.

LAURA   It's what we're good at. It's our collective term. There's a Whine of writers. And a Me of actors.

MILO	*(Makes note)* That's nice, we can use that.
DOBBSY	And a fifty pee of producers.
LAURA	Why a fifty pee?
DOBBSY	Many sided and two faced. You can use that too.
NAT	No we can't, that's an old joke.
LAURA	He's an old man.
MILO	I thought we were keeping gender politics out of this?
LAURA	I did. Those were ageist politics.
DOBBSY	You see how they gang up on me? If they tell an old joke it's *(Making air quotes)* 'retro.' I tell one and it's...
NAT	*(Air quotes)* 'Shit?'
DOBBSY	You'll be forty nine yourselves one day.
NAT	Ha!
MILO	Can we get back to business?
LAURA	What is business again, I've forgotten?
MILO	The line.
LAURA	Ah yes, the line. My queendom for a line!
MILO	Steady.
NAT	The rest of us leave our egos at the door, Laura should leave her nose.
LAURA.	I can't help it, I have a bi-polar disorder. How can I write comedy unless I'm buzzing?

DOBBSY   *(Derisively)* Cocaine! When I wrote for Mr.
           Pastry we got a pot of tea and a Penguin.

           Nat looks puzzled.

MILO   Laura, be careful. You've run out of warnings.

           *Laura looks miffed. Dobbsy remarks this news
           with interest.*

MILO   Now, let's try again. Annie is in bed. She's
           feeling neglected. Pete looks up from his -

           Nat has his hand up.

MILO   Yes, Nat?

NAT   Mr Pastry's been dead for yonks. How can
           Dobbsy be forty nine?

DOBBSY   I was a prodigy. I started writing at school.

NAT   Who with, Keats and Disraeli?

DOBBSY   *(Angrily)* I am not fucking old!

MILO   Enough!

           Silence.

MILO   Maybe that's the trouble. Maybe you've all
           forgotten what it is that pays our salaries.
           In that case, let me remind you.

MILO   *(Milo picks up script)* This is the Shroud Of
           Turin. What is it?

ALL   *(Wearily, except Dobbsy)* The Shroud of Turin.

MILO   Dobbsy?

DOBBSY   I'm not saying that. Stuff like that is so...
           American.

MILO   Okay. It's the start of a new series and I've
        been trying to keep a mellow mood, but...
        Dobbsy, where do you live?

DOBBSY You know where I live, Fulham.

MILO   Near Wyfold Road?

DOBBSY It's round the corner, why?

MILO   That's where the Jobcentre is.

        Dobbsy looks at Milo.

MILO   It's up to you.

DOBBSY *(Mutters)* The Shroud of Turin.

MILO   Anybody know why we call it that?

DOBBSY *(Angrily)* Because it's fake!

MILO   No, Dobbsy, because it contains our lifeblood.

        (He smooths the script) This is the dog eared,
        somewhat battered pilot script for our show,
        'Annie's People.'

        (Reads) 'Warm, wryly amusing tales of a
        modern divorced woman, struggling to get by.'
        Go on, everybody, reach out. Reach out and
        touch our show.

        They all reach out, touch it, except Dobbsy.

DOBBSY Yech!

MILO   Dobbsy.

DOBBSY You think I'm old? Well I'm old enough to
        know one thing: we stole our format from
        the Mary Tyler Moore show!

NAT   What's he gibbering about?

LAURA   Who's Mary Tyler Moore?

DOBBSY   *(To Milo)* Who's Mary Tyler..? There, you see
         what I'm up against?

MILO   You're up against the future. And you're
         standing in the way.

DOBBSY   Sure, like Crime and Punishment stood in the
         way of Heat magazine.

MILO   Dobbsy, there's only one unforgivable sin in
         our industry – and yes, I've learned to use
         phrases like 'in our industry' and 'water cooler
         moments' without blushing to the roots of my
         hair –

DOBBSY   And what roots! What hair!

MILO   And that sin is no longer to be useful. Take
         my advice, stay useful.

DOBBSY   *(Glowering huffily)* I can't help telling the
         truth.

MILO   This is television, try.

         Laura rises.

MILO   Laura, where are you going?

LAURA   I can't sit at this table any more. I don't feel
         good about myself or this show.

NAT   Did we really steal the format? That's so crap.

MILO   We did not steal the format, we liberated the
         format and re-energised it for today.

NAT   We did, we stole the format.

         Nat rises.

MILO   Nat, what are you doing?

NAT   It's catching. Now I feel bad about myself. To think I quit a law degree for this.

DOBBSY   Take yourself to court. Sue yourself for Plagiarism!

MILO   Laura, Nat, please sit down.

Laura and Nat share a glance. They remain standing, defiantly.

MILO   Team, may I remind you that in television, there is no such thing as theft. There are only wider ripples on the pond of truth.

LAURA   I hate this business.

MILO   Then you hate yourself. Television is a reflection of life, ergo if you hate television, you hate life.

NAT   Can we talk about me now please?

MILO   Guys, the choice is yours. Come hell or high water, with or without any writer in this room, there will be a series three of 'Annie's People.' And it will be a great series three. Do I make myself clear?

LAURA   *(Shrugs)* S'pose.

MILO   Good. Laura, please sit.

Laura sits.

MILO   Where are your feet?

LAURA   Under the table.

MILO   And are you staying with your feet?

Laura nods, reluctantly.

MILO   Nat?

They look at Nat. He sighs.

NAT   Another keen jawed idealist, lost to criminal justice.

Nat sits.

LAURA   You don't understand. I wanna do good work. Something special. Something like –

DOBBSY   *(Anticipating)* The Office! Yeh yeh, heard it.

Laura glares at Dobbsy.

MILO   Team, for every glittering success like The Office, there are fifty other shows on television. Average shows. Worthy shows. But shows that couldn't get wet if it was raining awards.

NAT   And after that fifty, there's us, right?

MILO   Correctamundo. Laura has decided to stay with her feet. Let's hear it for Laura's feet everyone.

Milo claps, forcefully. They join him, half heartedly.

DOBBSY   I've got feet too!

NAT   We know you do. Just keep them stuck in your mouth like always.

MILO   No, no, let's hear it for Dobbsy's feet too. In fact, let's hear it for everyone's feet! Come on! Come on!

(Self conscious whooping.) And are all our feet now present and correct?

ALL   Yes.

MILO	Then let's try again to walk the line – together!
NAT	What was the line?
MILO	*(Sighs)* Annie's in bed. She's feeling neglected. Pete looks up from his laptop. Pete says to Annie –

Door opens, suddenly. Cy leans in.

CY	Got room for a little 'un?

Laughter. Such timing.

MILO	Comedy, comedy! Come in, Cy.

Cy enters with Addy, a young black boy.

CY	Everybody, this is Addy. He's doing work experience. He'd like to join our team.
MILO	He would? How did Addy even find our team?
ADDY	Cy, Mr. Kellow, met my mum in a club on Saturday night, then they –
CY	Enough.

	(Addy shuts up. Cy nudges him.) Do the flattery.
ADDY	Just for a week. My whole family watch your show. My Gran, My Aunt Mo, we all love Annie's Song.
CY	People.
ADDY	Annie's People.
MILO	That was flattery?
CY	It's the best you've heard. So what do you say?
MILO	Well, team?

NAT	I'm not sure...
LAURA	Me neither.
DOBBSY	A Writers Room is sacrosanct. The public should never be admitted.
CY	Have a heart, he's ethnic.
	(To Addy) Do your 'raw kid who just deserves a break' look.
	Addy, makes a self conscious attempt to smile appealingly. Nat, Laura, Dobbsy look doubtful.
MILO	Okay. Young man, we'll give you a trial.
DOBBSY	Objection!
NAT	We haven't started yet.
ADDY	No, that's fair, a trial's cool.
MILO	Fine. So here's what we're working on. Annie's at home in bed. She's feeling amorous. Pete looks up from his laptop. Pete says 'The writer is like God. He –
	(Nod to Laura) or she – creates everything, yet his –
LAURA	Or her –
MILO	Existence is constantly questioned. What devastatingly witty comeback does Annie hit him with in reply?
	Everybody looks at Addy. He's intimidated.
ADDY	Uh.
MILO	Anything?
ADDY	Um.

CY	*(To Addy)* I don't want to labour the point but you're black. Cheerfulness is supposed to be born right in you people.
ADDY	I can't help it. Everybody's watching. I'm like... Tongue tied. Sorry.
MILO	Relax, Addy.
	(To team) Comments?
NAT	I think 'Uh,' 'Um' said it all really.
LAURA	Seconded. It's going to be a long week.
MILO	Dobbsy?
DOBBSY	Me? I loved him!
	(Dobbsy leans back in his chair, grabs his groin, macho fashion.) Competition... bring it on!
MILO	*(To Addy)* Young man, welcome to the Writer's Room.
	Addy smiles thinly.

SCENE 5

Int. day. (day 1) outside Cy's office.

Milo knocks, enters.

MILO	Can I see you?
	(Milo enters. Cy raises his hands in surrender.)
CY	Okay, I admit it. I'm screwing his mother. That's what I get for following my dick to Peckham! It's only a week, I swear it.
MILO	Relax, it isn't that.

CY   It's not me? No blame?

MILO   Not a thing.

CY   I feel an attack of confidence. Fire away.

MILO   It's funny you should say that.

CY   Fire...? Who'd you want out?

           (Defensively) Not Laura. That girl hates
           herself, she'll be a great comedy writer!
           If she'd only turn dyke, and wear a burka
           she'd tick all the right cultural boxes.
           Say it isn't Laura.

MILO   It isn't Laura.

CY   Nat then?

MILO   Not Nat.

CY   Not Nat or Laura.

           (Realisation) Not...

MILO   I'm afraid so. He's bad for team morale.

CY   Of course he is, that's his function. Dobbsy's
           the team ginger man. Acerbic but loveable.

MILO   Not any more. Not since Laura.

CY   Our ginger man is a woman?

MILO   She's developed. I've seen it coming.

CY   Developed? My God, what's happening here? I
           go to Montreaux for five minutes, I do the
           decent thing, I vote for those ludicrous gypsy
           nations, even though their humour stinks.
           When I come back my token female writer's
           sprouted balls.

MILO   It isn't that Laura growing balls, it's that Dobbsy's losing his.

CY   I can't believe I'm hearing this. You're asking me to fire Dobbsy. I can't fire Dobbsy.

MILO   You're the producer. If you can't fire Dobbsy, who can?

Cy looks at Milo.

MILO   Oh no, not me.

CY   Well I can't do it. If I fire Dobbsy, I'll be the oldest man on the show.

MILO   It is what it is.

CY   Don't be so smug. I could fire Dobbsy and I could fire me. Then you'd be the oldest man on the show.

MILO   Nice move. But I could outflank you with my masterplan.

CY   What masterplan?

MILO   Sex change.

CY   Go on.

MILO   I hang up my balls – or give give them to Laura. Then I'd be the only transsexual on the team. And you wouldn't dare upset the tranny vote because sexual deviants account for thirteen percent of our audience.

CY   Seventeen, after the ep with the dog... I'm telling you, Milo, we should bring in more Livestock! Pigs, cripples, dwarves! And just watch the public slavver!

They look at each other, sad, desperate men together.

CY   Listen to us. What's to become of us?

MILO   *(Shrugs)* What becomes of everybody? If we're lucky, we'll do eight series then we'll implode. We'll pass our days dreaming of Hollywood from cafes in Cricklewood. One of us will die and there'll be a reunion. Then another. And each time we meet our hair will be greyer and the reunions will be smaller. And you know the strange thing?

CY   What?

MILO   The strange thing is when we look back, we'll glorify this present moment, right here right now, as being the best time of our lives.

CY   Comedy comedy!

MILO   Comedy, comedy!

They laugh. Cy opens his arms. They hug. Cy's face darkens.

CY   Milo?

MILO   Hmm?

CY   *(Plaintively)* When did normal Englishmen start to hug instead of just shaking hands like we used to?

MILO   Just do it. The room might be bugged.

They finish the hug.

CY   I'll make a deal with you, Milo. In a few years time, when fate's handing us our awards, strokes, heart attacks, malignant tumours, whichever one of us dies first should try to get his comedy timing right, Don't you think?

MILO   How'd you mean?

CY   Well say 'Annie' made one of those Hundred Best Sitcom lists on Beeb One. If one of us were to croak on air! On a drip! In a hospice! Patting a one eared dog or midget! The public would eat it up! Overnight we'd be more than just another show, we'd be a National Treasure, we'd be loved!

MILO   Only on Beeb One?

CY   Or Channel Three or Four.

MILO   Not Two or Five?

CY   No way. I'm not dying for anything under a twenty percent audience share.

MILO   I love working with you, Cy. I always know where I am.

CY   (Sniffs his armpit) It's the stench of desperation, isn't it, I just can't shake it off!

            They laugh, look at each other, beaming fondly.

            What a team!

MILO   You said it! So what'll you do about Dobbsy?

            They stop laughing. Smiles vanish.

CY   What'll I do? You want him out. It's your team.

MILO   My team? You hired every one of us!

CY   *(Incredulous)* Oh, and that makes me your
            boss? Just because I earn twice your salary
            and can hire and fire you? What a quaint
            world view you scribblers entertain!

MILO   Cy, do your job.

CY   Oh sure! And what if I bump him and he's
            distraught? What if he takes a running jump
            off the top floor and splats onto the concrete!
            Have you thought what that means? It means
            a big red face for me! I can't do it, Milo.

MILO   Dobbsy isn't cutting it!

CY   Look, I hired Dobbsy, you fire him! Haven't
            you the decency to meet me halfway?

MILO   He has to go!

CY   Then you sack him!

MILO   Alright I will... I will!

            Milo exits, slamming the door.

SCENE 6

Outside Cy's office. Continuous.

*Milo stands, panting, hands shaking. Dobbsy appears
by him. Dobbsy proffers sweets.*

DOBBSY   Pan drop?

            *Milo takes a mint. He looks at Dobbsy's
            trusting, smiling face. Milo frowns, his resolve
            weakening, visibly.*

SCENE 7

Int. night. (Day 1) Milo's house. An ordinary terraced house in Chiswick. Bedroom.

Milo is in bed with his wife, Faith. They're making love.

FAITH   He wants you to do what?

MILO   He wants me to sack Dobbsy.

FAITH   Dobbsy's an old man. The show is all he has. What spineless low life rat came up with that one?

MILO   The one you're making love to.

MILO   *(They stop making love.)* Don't look at me like that, you don't know what it's like in there. We're ruthless men who kill for chuckles.

FAITH   When I married you, you were nice.

MILO   I was young then. I've been steeled in the crucible of the guffaw.

FAITH   Look, don't let's talk about work. Do me a favour, keep banging away for a while, will you?

MILO   *(Sighs)* When you put it like that...

             They resume making love. Faith starts to get into it. Milo stops.

MILO   It's no good.

FAITH   What's the matter?

MILO   Usual trouble. I choke when I get to the punch line.

FAITH	God, your insides must be like a Creme Egg by now.
MILO	Sublimation. It's all going into my novel.
FAITH	All of it? You'd never get the pages open.
MILO	Groan.
FAITH	There, you've had the first groan, I bags the second, what'd you say?

She reaches for Milo.

MILO	Shh!
FAITH	What is it?
MILO	Is that them?

They listen. we hear the heavy thump of a base line from next door's stereo.

MILO	It is, it's them.
FAITH	Ignore it.
MILO	I can't, it goes right through me.
FAITH	There's an irony.
MILO	I'm, telling you, Faith, one of these nights I'm going to blow!
FAITH	Just not tonight though, eh?
MILO	I mean it. Look at my hands. Look at the effect he has on me.
FAITH	Then do something about it. Go next door and knock his block off!
MILO	Too big. How about I knock her block off?

Raucous female laughter from next door.

FAITH   Get in the queue, behind me.

MILO   What do you want, Faith? From life I mean?

FAITH   You know what I want. Go further in publishing. Bigger house. Children.

MILO   I meant... spiritually.

FAITH   Children.

MILO   I knew you'd say that.

FAITH   But it's not an issue.

She suckles a Tellytubby at her breast. Milo looks glum.

FAITH   You know what you need? You need to quit whining and confront your problems.

MILO   You're right. I'll start with that big lank haired in-breed next door.

FAITH   You will? Go, tiger.

MILO   Watch me.

Milo rises, opens a drawer on a chest. He holds up two sets of coloured ear plugs.

MILO   Cerise or jonquil?

FAITH   Jonquil.

MILO   *(Proffers)* That's a relief. Yellow is so unmanly.

They put in their ear plugs. Milo turns out his bedside light. Faith looks fed up.

MILO   Night, Faith. *(Silence)*

           Faith?

FAITH   What?

MILO   What am I going to do about Dobbsy?

FAITH   Bring him home, I'll fuck him to death.

MILO   Thanks, Faith.

FAITH   Pleasure.

Faith turns out her bedside light. Milo broods.

WHAT HAPPENS NEXT?
CAN YOU HAVE THE LAST LAUGH?

Being Dad

by Trix Worrell

© BBC

TRIX WORRELL

Trix is a writer, composer and director with a selection of awards under his belt: including a Lifetime Achievement Award from the Royal Television Society in 1998.

His writing credits include: on TV, Desmonds, the Cosby Show, What You Looking At and Porkpie and on the big screen, Meet The Clan with Pam Greer. He has also written the script for Puff Daddy when he was the presenter for the MTV Europe Music Awards! Recently he has been working on an album and setting up a production company both entitled 'A Box Of Trix'. They will showcase new musical and writing talent.

SCENE 1

Int. bedroom. Morning.

This is a typical boys bedroom circa 1990.

There are posters on the wall of semi clad babes, Tottenham Football Club and musical icons of the time. This room is really a throw back to that age. In the corner of one wall, a gallant attempt has been made to redecorate. The paper stripper is jammed between the wall and the paper and a ladder lies idle. The room has that temporary feel about it as two bags overflow with clothes. Simon Williams – black early thirties – lies in bed. His hands are in prayer and eyes are closed.

SIMON   *(Accent a combination of London and Patois)* Lord, God, Jah, Allah, Geezer or man who run tings. I still hate doing this praying business, but it seems to work and I'll try anything once. Don't let me gamble for one more day. I know you have 'nuff tings to worry about, and my little request won't bring world peace but since you create this place has there ever been peace? Don't answer that. It's been two hundred and seventy two days plus change since I gambled and lost everything I had on the two thirty at Kempton. I know that everyday the odds are staked against me, but make today an even day, not an odd one because I've got a job interview this afternoon. OK that's me done.

    (Patios) 'nuff re-spect, easy God.

    (He makes the peace sign) Peace.

    He turns over and goes back to sleep pulling the duvet over his head.

A beat.

The alarm clock rings. It's ten o'clock. He sticks out a hand and turns it off. Next to the clock he picks up a coin and sleepily, hauls himself up.

SIMON   *(Yawning)* Heads, I get out of bed. Tails, I stay for another hour.

He flips the coin. Catches it and places it on the back of his hand covered by his other hand. He screws his face and looks at the result through one eye. Sighs and 'kisses his teeth' – loudly.

SCENE 2

Int. Kitchen/living room. Morning.

Simon, wearing a spectacularly bright dressing gown with Circus Circus Las Vegas logo on the back, the rest of the gown is covered with playing cards, roulette wheels. He stands in front of an open overhead cupboard in a kitchen, which dates back to the early eighties. Inside are several plates and two boxes of breakfast cereal, one more appealing than the other, he looks at the porridge and screws his face up. He sighs at his options and then closes his eyes and plays an elimination game.

SIMON   *(Closing his eyes)* Ippa, dippa, dashion, my apperation. How many people waiting at the station? 'Four'. One, two, three. Four. You are not it.

He opens his eyes to see which cereal he has chosen. It's the least attractive.

SIMON   Best of three.

SCENE 3

Simon is sitting at the table, eating from a bowl of what we believe is porridge. It's solid and unappetising. He screws his face up as he takes one more bite of the chewy substance. A mobile phone rings and he answers it.

SIMON   Hello?

VOICE   Wha-appen blood?

SIMON   How many times do I have to tell you Jay I don't bet any more.

JAY   Yeah I know but this is a dead cert. Sobriety 20-1. Three o'clock Sandown.

SIMON   No way, eleven o'clock, Simon.

With that he turns the phone off and shakes his head. He picks up the television remote control and switches it on. We hear the sound of horse racing. He switches it off again. He picks up another spoonful of porridge. He looks at it and then smiles as he spies some cups by the sink. He aims the spoon at them and then flicks a ball of porridge. Crash.

SIMON   Yes!

The door bell rings. Simon gets up.

SCENE 4

Int. hall. Morning.

Simon opens the door out onto a good looking black woman in her early thirties. This is Yvonne. Standing next to her their twelve year old son Sean, who looks down, he is smartly dressed in sports awareness clothing – Adidas track suit and hoody and Nike trainers. Simon looks on speechless.

A beat.

YVONNE   *(Peeved)* Well aren't you going to say hello?

SIMON   *(Still stunned)* Hello Yvonne... Sean?

YVONNE   Your father remembers our names. That's
a start.

*Simon looks at Sean, who smiles back. With
that she barges past Simon and makes her
way into the house. Sean, without looking at
him, shrugs his shoulders and follows her in.*

SCENE 5

Int. kitchen / living room. Morning.

*Sean sits quietly on the sofa as Yvonne and Simon pace up
and down.*

YVONNE   I was watching that Batman climb the front
of Buckingham Palace, for Fathers 4 Justice.
Sean said if he was really doing it because
he wants to see his kids why is he hiding his
face. I thought I know another father who
doesn't show his face.

SIMON   That's because you said you didn't want to
see me.

YVONNE   That's because...

(Whispering not wanting Sean to hear)...
you lost our house. Most people lose mobile
phones or keys, you lose our house.

SIMON   I know, I said I'm sorry.

YVONNE   I'm still pissed. I said I didn't want to see
you. I didn't stop you from seeing your son.

SIMON	You moved away.
YVONNE	We were homeless. We had no choice.
SIMON	I haven't seen you for seven years and we are rowing as if it were yesterday. I don't need this, I'm going for a job in few hours and trying to sort myself out. I haven't gambled for two hundred and thirty days and eleven hours.
YVONNE	I'm glad to hear those seven years wasn't wasted. I thought I'd be all right seeing you again.
	With that Yvonne tries to hold it in. Simon moves towards her and gives her a cuddle.
YVONNE	*(Stiffening)* Don't touch me.
	(Softening and giggling) Especially there, you know how much... Mmm
	She pulls away from him and slaps him.
SIMON	What was that for?
YVONNE	For still knowing how to get round me.
	Simon smiles. She slaps him again.
SIMON	And that?
YVONNE	For giving up gambling.
SIMON	Of all people I thought you'd be pleased.
YVONNE	Why couldn't you do that for us and for him?
SIMON	*(Looking at his watch)* I really am going for an interview.
YVONNE	Good, I won't stay.

She walks over to Sean and gives him a hug.

YVONNE Bye son.

SIMON What do you mean? What's going on?

YVONNE Oh did I forget to tell you, Sean wants to live with his Dad. He needs male influence now. I can't teach him that. He wants to talk to him about male tings, like girls, gangs, guns and all that peer pressure that young black men are under. It's your turn Simon. I'm Audi.

She starts to leave.

SIMON *(Flabbergasted)* What! How is this going to work?

YVONNE *(Irony)* I'll visit at weekends or when ever I feel like it. Sounds familiar?

SIMON *(Lost for words and trying desperately not to reject his son)* But...

YVONNE I'm sure you'll work it out. You have to, otherwise Sean will have to throw you out.

With that Sean smiles.

SIMON What do mean throw me out?

YVONNE Didn't I say? Sean owns the house now. It's in trust but he'll legally own it when he's eighteen.

SIMON What? He's twelve!

YVONNE It's a long story, but I'll keep it simple so that you can understand.

(She takes a deep breath and talks without pausing) You know when your Father was going back and forwards to St Lucia saying he

was building his house, how he had to be there because he didn't trust the builders. Well the thing is he wasn't just building a house, he was building another family too and the person we couldn't trust wasn't the builders it was him. It all came out when your Mum went back home to bury him. They all came out all three of them.

SIMON   Three!

YVONNE   All different mothers, same result they all want some money. So your mum decided she didn't want to lose her house, sound familiar? She was smart; she transferred the house to her only grandson, your son.

Simon is stunned, she looks into her handbag and pulls out a cheque book and hands it to Simon.

SIMON   What am I...

YVONNE   From now on you'll pay rent, which will go into Sean's account. Let's call it his college account.

She starts to gasp for air, and composes herself.

SIMON   Why didn't she tell me?

YVONNE   She don't trust you Simon. She wasn't sure what you would do with the house.

Yvonne gives Sean another cuddle, as Simon stares into space.

SIMON   *(Totally bewildered, trying to retrace his day)* How can this be? This was supposed to be an even day. I woke up I didn't even stay in bed today... I shouldn't have eaten the porridge...

YVONNE   *(Kissing him)* Look after your Dad, looks like he's going to be sick.

SEAN   Yes Mum. Bye Mum.

YVONNE   Bye my little man.

           With that Yvonne walks out of the room. Simon runs after her.

SCENE 6

Int/ext. house. Peckham. Morning.

Yvonne opens the door and is about to leave.

SIMON   *(Still in a daze)* Is there anything I should know about Sean?

YVONNE   Like whether or not he wets the bed, or is he housetrained. You'll just have to find out won't you?

SIMON   So when are you coming back?

YVONNE   When he's eighteen.

SIMON   *(Panicking)* But that's...

YVONNE   Too long? Welcome to parenting, it's not just for Christmas and birthdays it's for life.

SIMON   What about school?

YVONNE   That's for you to know and me to find out.

SIMON   I don't have your mobile?

YVONNE   Email me on 'I'm on holiday dot com'. Speak to your son; that's a novelty. He's got my digits.

We hear the sound of a car horn. Yvonne turns round and waves at Vanessa, a pretty blonde woman in her late twenties sitting in a gleaming BMW convertable.

SIMON   *(Showing interest)* Who's that?

YVONNE   That. Is not your type.

She playfully slaps him.

SIMON   *(Worried)* Why did you do that? It's an odd number now, three times. It's my even day today. You need to do it again.

She looks at him and shakes her head.

He closes his eyes expecting. This time she is about to it with menace but changes her mind as she looks at the man she once loved. She pats him on the cheek.

SIMON   Thanks.

She walks towards the car, she knows he is watching and she swings those hips. She climbs into the car, gives the woman a hug. Looks back at Simon who is standing by the door. She points down to a number of suitcases. Simon scoops them up.

SCENE 7

Int. kitchen / living room. Morning.

Simon staggers into the living room carrying three large heavy bags. He drops them onto to the floor. Now he can see the room and the sight of Sean laid out on the sofa about to smoke a spliff, horrifies him.

SIMON   What the hell do you think you are doing?

SEAN   *(Calm. Street language)* Having a spliff innit.

SIMON   Not over my dead body you're not. No smoking of any kind in this house.

SEAN   You've been dead to me for a long time, you get me.

SIMON   I'm alive now. You're only twelve and you're smoking.

SEAN   *(Putting away the lighter)* I don't smoke. I was just seeing how far I could push you. You get me?

     Simon clicks his fingers. Sean hands over the joint. Simon smells it.

SIMON   *(Pocketing it)* Skunk. I'm confiscating it, you get me?

SEAN   *(Knowingly)* Yeah right. You're going to smoke it aint you Dad

SIMON   Call me Si Dad sounds so...

SEAN   Responsible.

SIMON   *(Wry smile)* I thought your Mum left the building. OK It's not that. I just thought that since you clearly are more grown up than I gave you credit for. I'd like it if you called me Si that's all, like mates, you know.

SEAN   *(Dismissive)* Mates! How old are you? How can I be your mate? We don't even speak the same language. You get me. You're my Dad Simon.

SIMON	I'm your Dad, who's also called Simon. I'd just liked to be called Simon, that's all.
SEAN	I get it, you're one of those.
SIMON	One of what?
SEAN	Don't want to grow up Dads. The ones you see at the Raves trying to check the young girls. You're one of those you're as young as the girl you're feeling Dads ain't it? There's a word for that. Paedophile you get me and I thought you only had a gambling problem.
SIMON	I know you are angry with me.
SEAN	*(Flippant)* Nah this ain't angry, you ain't seen me angry yet cous' I'm scared of myself when I'm angry, you get me?
SIMON	You telling me this because?
SEAN	Mum found it difficult when I got vexed and tried to voice my opinion, she said it's aggressive. You get me.
SIMON	She used to be the same to me. You get me?
SEAN	Rewind, what's with the street talk all of a sudden.
SIMON	*(Patois)* Are we on the streets now? Don't talk to me like that then you get me. D'is street chat you ah g'wan wid is just progression from the when I was your age. *(Mimicking Sean)* You get me?
SEAN	Why are you such a crap Dad?
SIMON	*(Taking time to answer)* I just don't think I was ready for it.

SEAN	Didn't you want me then?
SIMON	*(Realising he made a mistake)* Course I did.
SEAN	You've got a funny way of showing it.
SIMON	*(Sincerely)* It wasn't about you. I thought I could deal with it all but I couldn't, you know. I just got grief. From your Mum, her Mum, and my Mum.

He shakes his head. A beat.

SEAN	That was a real Trisha moment.
	(Hand on chest sincerely) I'm feeling it, you get me.
SIMON	*(Insulted)* Man, I'm too good looking to be on Trisha.
SEAN	You're right there. Forget the lie detector, you have to pass some ugly test to be on her show, you get me.

They laugh for a moment and are suddenly aware that they are enjoying each other's company. Sean stops laughing so does Simon.

A beat.

SEAN	Do you think grief is what women give to men they love? Mum says she loves me but she still gives me grief. She used to give her other boyfriends grief too.
SIMON	It wasn't only me then, that's a relief. What other boyfriends?
SEAN	You don't want to know.
SIMON	You're probably right but I still want to know.

SEAN	Well nobody serious apart from Uncle Jay.
SIMON	*(Angry)* Jay? My mate Jay! He's not your uncle.
SIMON	I figured that out when he started sleeping with Mum. But they were all soft *(Looking at his Dad)*. I know what Mum means when she says that Vanessa is the only person she's met with balls.
SIMON	Vanessa?
SEAN	Her girlfriend?
SIMON	What sort of girlfriend?
SEAN	The stay over night sort.
SIMON	In the same bed sort?
SEAN	Put it this way, we lived in a two bedroom flat, I was in one bedroom Mum was in the other, I never saw Vanessa on the sofa bed.
SIMON	Your Mum is gay?
SEAN	She's happy. That's all that matters, You've seen her wheels with those alloys, and if my girl was driving around drop Bema I'd be well happy. So would you believe! And she got corn, she's got a house in Ibiza that's where they've gone for a week. I told Mum to hang onto her until I reach Ibiza.
SIMON	Wow they must be serious. How long have they been together?
SEAN	I don't know. I just saw the Lex.
SIMON	Lex?

SEAN	*(Look skywards)* Rolex man. I thought you said you're 'Street'.
SIMON	I am. Just that we're not on the streets now.
SEAN	Like I said, I just saw the Lex, you don't ask questions after that, you get me.
SIMON	Let's get you settled into your bedroom shall we?
	Sean gets up from the sofa and picks up a bag. They make their way up some stairs onto a landing with adjoining rooms.
SEAN	I want to stay in Granny and Grandad's bedroom.
SIMON	You can't.
SEAN	Why not? It's the biggest bedroom and I own it.
SIMON	But it's Granny and Grandad's.
SEAN	Grandad's dead and Granny is not coming back.
SIMON	How do you know that?
SEAN	She told me.
SIMON	How come she didn't tell me? She's my Mum.
SEAN	Because... You can't be trusted?
SIMON	*(Peeved. like a small child)* That's not true, Wait till I see Granny.
SEAN	That's all you're going to do. Wait to see her because she's in St Lucia and you're broke. You're always broke.
SIMON	Who told you that?

SEAN	Me. Judging from the crap Christmas presents you used to send me.

They stop outside chocolate brown door. Simon opens it. It's dark inside.

SIMON	This is your room.
SEAN	Man it smells old.

(Sean looks in) You sure it's got electricity.

Simon places the bags by the door.

SIMON	Yes, all you need to do is open the curtains.

With that Simon leaves Sean to it. We follow him as he makes way to the stairs.

We hear the curtains open.

SEAN	*(OOV. disappointing)* Oh man have you seen this wallpaper!! Ahhhhh!!

Simon smiles to himself.

SCENE 8

Int. kitchen/living room. Midday.

Sean and Simon look at each other there is a deadly silence.

SEAN	Can you cook?
SIMON	A little, you?
SEAN	A little too.
SIMON AND SEAN	Breakfast.

SIMON   I suppose that's something we've got in
             common. Why don't you tell me a little about
             yourself.

SEAN   Those suitcases we carried, that's me. Oh plus
             a new play station, an Ipod Vanessa bought
             me. Not enough designers' labels in my
             wardrobe, looking forward to having sex.

SIMON   *(Shocked)* Have you got a girlfriend?

SEAN   *(Boasting)* If I had one I wouldn't be looking
             forward to it would I.

SIMON   Thank god for that. Listen Sean I really
             think...

SEAN   *(Winding him up)* Don't worry I'll use a
             condom. Have you got any?

SIMON   No Sean!

SEAN   *(Laughing)* Just playing you. Want to
             know more?

SIMON   *(Unsure)* I think so.

SEAN   I like to get a good job... Have you got a job?

SIMON   *(Flustered)* Well no, but I've got an interview
             this afternoon.

SEAN   See don't look good does it. You're thirty and
             you don't have a job and your still living at
             home. Mum says that I need a male influence.
             Man I've got problems.

SIMON   I don't have anyone to blame but myself. I got
             myself in this situation. The thing is if you
             work hard and get decent grades and go to
             Uni, you'll get a good job at least stand as
             good a chance as the next man.

	(Looking at his watch) And if I don't get a move on I won't be getting any work.
SEAN	What time is your interview?
SIMON	Three o'clock.
	They look at the retro seventies clock on the wall. It reads 12.30.
SEAN	Where is it?
SIMON	Elephant and Castle.
SEAN	You've got plenty of time.
	A beat.
	Clock is deafening.
SEAN	So Dad why don't you tell me about yourself and what's been happening to you in the last seven years.
SIMON	Well...
	He starts to think.

SCENE 9

Int. kitchen diner. Mid day.

Fifteen minutes later Sean is doing sit ups with his legs tucked under the sofa.

| SIMON | I ere... |

SCENE 10

Int. kitchen diner. Afternoon.

Fifteen minutes later, Sean is cooking up a storm in the kitchen. Simon is now lying on the sofa hand on head trying to think.

SIMON   I'm trying to think...

SCENE 11

Int. kitchen diner. Lunch time.

Simon is sitting at the dining table as Sean presents a plate of food in front of him. Rice and peas and chicken plantain and sweet potatoes. Simon is trying to think as he tucks in, not commenting on the fact that Sean has cooked a gourmet dish.

SIMON   I really don't know...

SCENE 12

Int. kitchen diner. Lunch time.

Simon is washing up whilst Sean is stretched out on the sofa tired after his efforts. Simon is washing up. He turns round to Sean. It's now forty five minutes later.

SIMON   I've been to see Spurs quiet a lot.

SEAN   *(Too past it to care)* Great, that's wicked.

SIMON   Do you like them?

SEAN   No, Gooner mate, but at least we can talk about how much I hate Spurs. It's funny I wondered what I would say to you if I saw you again.

SIMON *(Feeling guilty)* Listen I'm sorry.

SEAN I'm not. This is heavy, my own house.

SIMON Not until you're eighteen.

SEAN Well you got some time before you have to find another place. How did you lose the house?

SIMON Didn't she tell you?

SEAN I wouldn't be asking.

SIMON Good point, if she aint I'm certainly not going to tell you.

The monotone 'grime' tune of Dizzee Rascal rings on Sean's mobile phone. Sean looks at the caller ID and ignores it. Simon is getting irritated by the ring tone.

SIMON Answer it or switch it off that rubbish.

SEAN *(Reluctantly answers it. Street)* Yes Dwayne what you saying?... Listen cous' don't talk no foolishness you hear 'bout bare dis and bare d'at, you get me... Dwayne, I can't I'm at my drum, south side... Yeah rare, rare, rare. I don't run from you, but I'm going to allow it you get me. You'll get your edge cous'! Dwayne? Dwayne?

Dwayne has hung up the phone. Sean looks angry and worried. Simon is concerned.

SIMON Who was that?

SEAN Wrong number.

SIMON Are you all right?

SEAN *(Distracted)* Yeah.

SIMON	*(Trying to be upbeat)* Why don't you help me pick out a suit for my interview?
SEAN	It's not one of those bonding things is it?
SIMON	Just thought it would give us something to talk about that's all.
	During the following dialogue we will see Simon walking into the living room wearing a series of different suits.
SEAN	OK, what sort of job is it?
SIMON	I don't want to talk about that.
SEAN	I thought you wanted to talk.
SIMON	I do, but I just want to talk about the job just in case I don't get it.
SEAN	I don't get it?
SIMON	Just call it superstition.
SEAN	How can you be superstitious about a job you haven't got yet?
SIMON	It's a gambling thing OK.
SEAN	Like today being an even day right?
SIMON	Right. It's what gets me through the day.
SEAN	That's cool with me. "Get you through the day".
	(Suspicious) It's not hereditary, this gambling thing is it?
SIMON	No.
SEAN	It's not contagious, like I heard people say that they caught the gambling bug.

SIMON	No it's not that sort of bug.
SEAN	What sort of illness is it, 'cause from the little I've seen of it you ain't all there, you get me. It's not that I'm dissing you.
SIMON	Well that's a start.
SEAN	Thinking about it all my friends' parents are messed up, separated divorce, no Dad, plus a lot of them are on drugs and stuff, Prozac and drink and that's just the middle class ones, you get me. The only one I know whose parents are sorted is Krish, they are Muslim and we keep being told how messed up that is. That's the suit. Yeah you look 'durty' in that.
SIMON	You like it then?

SCENE 13

Int/ext. house. Peckham. Day.

Sean is standing at the open door as Simon hovers nervously.

SIMON	*(Nervous)* Well here I go.
SEAN	Easy.
	He is about to set off when he spins round.
SIMON	Did I tell…
SEAN	Yeah, don't open the door to strangers
SIMON	You've got my mobile if…
SEAN	*(Sighing)* 07978 (etc)…
SIMON	OK. I'm off.
SEAN	Good.

SIMON	You sure the suit is OK?
SEAN	You're beginning to sound like my bitch now, man. What's wrong with you?
SIMON	*(Angry. He glares at Sean)* Don't ever talk to me like that, you hear me.
	Simon glares at Sean.
SEAN	What ever it is you're thinking of doing to me, don't 'cause I'll call Child Line.
	He flips out his phone. Simon shakes his head and walks away. Sean closes the door behind him. We stay with Simon as he walks down opens the gate and starts to walk away. *The front door opens.*
SEAN	Good luck!
	Sean smiles at Simon and gives him thumbs up.
SIMON	Thanks!

SCENE 14

Int. living room. Day.

Sean is standing the middle of the room with his arms outstretched.

SEAN	Yes my own drum.
	He starts to dance over to the fire place above is a stiff photo of his Gran and Grandad. *He picks it up and kisses each person.*
SEAN	Thank you Grandad, you dirty old man. A special kiss for you Granny, for being smart.
	He dives onto the sofa and stretches out.

SCENE 15

Ext. Walworth Road. Day.

Music over.

Simon walks into newsagents. We stay outside.

A beat.

He then comes out brandishing a copy of 'The Racing Post'.

He looks around suspiciously before he tucks it under his arm and walks off.

SCENE 16

Int. bus. Day.

Simon is studying the form. He has a pen in his hand as he circles a horse. We see that it is Sobriety.

SCENE 17

Int. living room. Day.

Sean is luxuriating on sofa with feet up. He is drinking coke and eating from a large bag of crisps. Playing with his PlayStation. He sighs heavily and beams as he is master of all he surveys.

SCENE 18

Ext. Elephant and Castle. Day.

Simon, gingerly walks past the bookmakers. The front door is open invitingly. He doubles back and loiters outside thinks about it and then walks off.

SCENE 19

Ext. Elephant and Castle. Day.

Simon is standing outside the bookies; inside the race is in the finale throws as those gathered cheer on their horse.

It's a cacophony of sound. We see Simon's eyes light up and as he is lured into the race.

SIMON   Come on Sobriety!

      A crowd has gathered as Simon becomes more and more animated. They look on curiously and can't help but be infected by Simon's enthusiasm.

SIMON   Come on Sobriety.

      (Orgasmic) Yes, yes, yes!!

      Simon starts to dance round he grabs the first girl he sees and kisses her.

GIRL   How much did you win?

SIMON   I didn't. That's the point.

      She is outraged. She slaps him across the face.

SIMON   Shit it's odd. Excuse me!!

      She sees him and starts to run. He looks at his watch takes a deep breath and walks into the bookies.

SCENE 20

Int. living room. Day.

Sean is playing a video game clearly bored.

A beat.

The door bell rings with a flourish. Sean's face lights up and he bounds to the door. We follow him as he reaches it. He stops dead as he recognises the voices on the other side of the door.

DWAYNE   OOV

              You sure this is it?

Sean ducks down, and start to slowly retreat. His phone rings – it's Dwayne. He curses under his breath, as he realises that they can hear his phone.

DWAYNE   OOV

              Sean open up!

Sean walks to the front door and opens it. Dwayne a large puppy type boy stands at the door dressed in the latest and best designer gear, Burberry hat, Adidas track, and Nike trainers. Elliot skinny white boy – also wearing sports awareness clothing and Parv an Asian boy dressed similarly accompany him.

WHAT HAPPENS NEXT?
CAN YOU HAVE THE LAST LAUGH?

Entry details

Rules

Please ensure that you have read, and agreed to the following rules and entrant's agreement. If you enter the competition we will take it that you have read, and agree to abide by, these rules.

The script must be:

- The ending to one of the eight sitcoms which have been written for The Last Laugh
- You/your writing team's own work, original and unpublished
- 10 minutes in duration
- Received by 5pm on Friday 6th May 2005. Entries received after this date will be disqualified.

You/your writing team must all be:

- Over 16 years of age, as at Friday 6th May 2005
- A UK resident
- Not a professional script writer
- Without a conviction which entails current imprisonment
- Not an employee of the BBC.

HOW TO ENTER

1) You can enter via our website
   www.bbc.co.uk/lastlaugh
   follow the instructions on the site.

or

2) Send one printed copy on single sides of A4 paper,
   to The Last Laugh, BBC Broadcasting House,
   Queen Margaret Drive, Glasgow, G12 8DG

Include a completed covering sheet with the information
requested below. If you are part of a team please complete
and sign one sheet per team member.

Please lay your sitcom out in the same format as the book.

    Name

    Home address

    Home phone number

    Mobile number (where applicable)

    Daytime contact number

    E Mail address (where applicable)

    Sitcom chosen

    I have read, and agree to abide by the competition

    rules and entrants agreement

    Signature

The BBC will only ever use your personal details for the
purposes of administering this competition, and will not
publish them or provide them to anyone without your
permission. If you would like to know more about the
BBC's privacy policy, please visit the website:

www.bbc.co.uk/privacy

VOLUNTARY INFORMATION

We would also like to know a little bit more about you, and why you have entered this competition. The following information requests are entirely voluntary and not answering them will not affect the judging of your story. The information will be treated in the strictest confidence.

- Your age as of entrance date
- Your sex Male/Female
- How did you hear about the competition?

    TV Show/website/print

    Radio/Last Laugh Book

    Other – please specify

- Ethnic origin

    Asian/Asian British

    Black/Black British

    Middle/Near Eastern

    Mixed Ethnic Group

    White

    Other – please specify

- Do you have ambitions to be a professional script writer?
- Why have you chosen to enter the competition?
- Why did you select the sitcom you have chosen?

ENTRANT'S AGREEMENT

By submitting a script you grant to the BBC a perpetual, royalty-free, non-exclusive, license to sub-edit, publish, make available and distribute your script throughout the World on the Last Laugh website, BBC television and any BBC media now known or hereafter invented.

In submitting a script, you agree that if you are selected as one of the finalists you will work with the BBC production team for the production of a proposed associated TV series. The finalists must be available for a limited amount of filming, may be required to take part in publicity and be able to travel to UK locations during summer 2005. The BBC cannot guarantee that any programme will be made or transmitted or that any finalist will be included in a programme.

The BBC does not accept any responsibility for late or lost entries. Proof of sending is not proof of receipt.

Only one entry into the competition will be accepted per person/writing team. People/teams found to have entered the ending of more than one sitcom will be disqualified.

Entries must be the original work of the entrant/entrants and not defame any person or corporate body or infringe or breach copyright.

Please make us aware of any non-spent convictions.

No entry can be returned.

Entries must be within the boundaries of acceptable taste, language and decency.

The entries will be judged by a professional team of readers and experts who will select a short-list of winning entries for each sitcom, on the basis of their originality and appropriateness in providing an ending. The author will make the final decision from the short-list. The BBC's decision is final and no correspondence will be entered into.

All stories may be published on the Last Laugh website on BBCi.

Frequently Asked Questions

HOW LONG SHOULD MY SCRIPT BE?

The ten minute ending to the script should be approximately 2,300 words. This is the word count you should aim for; different scripts will have more pauses/scene changes and therefore fewer words, and vice versa.

We will not disqualify you for a longer word count but your script, when read aloud, must last for 10 minutes. However, we know that scripts are tricky to judge in length so we won't be worried about the odd minute either way.

AM I A PROFESSIONAL SCRIPT WRITER?

If, in the past tax year, you earned more than 49% of your income (as shown on your tax return) from writing scripts (of any kind e.g. comedy/drama/documentary) then for the purposes of this competition you are a professional script writer and cannot enter.

HOW MANY PEOPLE CAN BE IN A WRITING TEAM?

A writing team can involve no more than 2 people, both of whom must meet the entrants' requirements. Once you have completed an entry form with the names of those in the team you cannot change these names.

WILL YOU ACKNOWLEDGE RECEIPT OF MY ENTRY?

Online entries – if you provide an e-mail address you will be sent an e-mail confirming we have received your script. If you don't provide an e-mail address then you will not receive a confirmation from us.

Typed entries – if you include a stamped addressed envelope then we will post it back to you when we have received your entry.

If you don't include an envelope then unfortunately we cannot confirm receipt. If you send your entry via Special or Recorded Delivery we cannot guarantee that entries will be signed for.

MORE QUESTIONS?

If there is anything else you would like to know, please email us at:

thelastlaugh@bbc.co.uk

or write to us at:

The Last Laugh, BBC Broadcasting House, Queen Margaret Drive, Glasgow, G12 8DG

THE PRIZE

One of the sitcoms will be made into a pilot. The choice will be made by Stuart Murphy, the channel contoller.

The eight winners will go to a masterclass day with some top sitcom bods.

Top 10 Tips

1) The main aim of a sitcom is to make your audience laugh.

2) Make sure you have a genuine laugh every three to four lines.

3) Make sure the characters are believable, even in sitcom world. Keep their actions within the realms of possibility.

4) Work out what you want from each scene, make it happen and then get out of it – don't hang around.

5) Show, don't tell. Show us the humour, the situation and the characters.

6) The final third should offer a conclusion, or resolution, to the plot or sub-plot. Don't introduce new places, plots or characters – unless you think it's absolutely essential.

7) Tailor your sitcom to your market – think who might find the beginning funny and write the ending with them in mind.

8) Keep your writing in the same vein as the original writer – you are completing a sitcom, not demonstrating how weird and wacky you can be.

9) Don't be afraid to keep re-writing until you're really, really happy with your work.

10) The last rule is that there are NO RULES.

Glossary

This is not a definitive list but it might help you when you're writing your ending.

beat – a one count pause in the speech or action. It can also be described as a plot point within your story structure.

cut to – a rapid switch to a different location, time of day, character or view etc. It can also refer to an immediate transition between scenes.

dialogue – the words spoken by your characters.

draft – a completed version of your script which then may be rewritten, revised or polished.

exposition – important background information for the events of your story.

ext. (exterior) – To be found in the scene heading specifying that the action is taking place outside

general view (g.v.) – general views of location/details of location to establish where the scene is.

int. (interior) – To be found in the scene heading specifying that the action is taking place inside.

out of vision (o.o.v.) – dialogue or sound that takes place out of view. This can be used when the characters are in other rooms – or speaking but not seen at that point by the audience. This is also sometimes referred to as o.s. (off screen).

p.o.v. (point of view) – the perspective from a particular character in your script.

scene – the section of drama in your script where an event occurs in one location, moving your story forward, usually during a certain amount of time.

subplot – the secondary events in your story that merge with the main story.

synopsis – a brief summary of your story told in present tense. This is usually two to three paragraphs in length.

voice over (V.O) – a character's voice heard during a scene where the character is not shown.